SO YOU THINK YOU'RE A NEW YORK RANGERS FAN?

STARS, STATS, RECORDS, AND MEMORIES FOR TRUE DIEHARDS

BY STEVE ZIPAY

SPORTS PUBLISHING

Sports Publishing books may be purchased in bulk at special discounts for sales promotion, corporate gifts, fund-raising, or educational purposes. Special editions can also be created to specifications. For details, contact the Special Sales Department, Sports Publishing, 307 West 36th Street, 11th Floor, New York, NY 10018 or sportspubbooks@skyhorsepublishing.com.

Sports Publishing® is a registered trademark of Skyhorse Publishing, Inc.®, a Delaware corporation.

Visit our website at www.sportspubbooks.com.

10 9 8 7 6 5 4 3 2 1

Library of Congress Cataloging-in-Publication Data is available on file.

Cover design by Tom Lau
Cover photo credit: Associated Press

ISBN: 978-1-68358-078-2
Ebook ISBN: 978-1-68358-079-9

Printed in the United States of America

Contents

Introduction

*"We all have our time machines, don't we? Those
that take us back are memories . . . And those
that carry us forward . . . are dreams."*
—*H.G. Wells*

To be honest, this isn't meant to be a definitive trivia book.

Consider it a challenge for those who have memories, and
for those who have dreams.

After all, with almost a century in the archives, the sweep-
ing Rangers saga resembles a river rushing by with names and
faces and stories and lights and shadows: Thousands of games,
hundreds of players, dozens of coaches and general managers,
four Stanley Cups, and yes, some seasons to forget.

That's a lot of territory to cover.

And really, the generational history of the Rangers is both
a crowd-share and immensely personal.

From those who remember going to the stately, smoky
Madison Square Garden on Eighth Avenue and 49th Street
wearing dark hats and ties, to the youngsters who were tossed a
puck in warmups from a player and will never, ever, forget that
evening, this collection is for you.

For those who first listened to games on transistor radios or
those who have watched on television or online, this is for you.

For those who laced up skates on a city or suburban rink or a nearby pond and imagined scoring a game-winning goal and raised their hands skyward among drifting snowflakes— or those who played roller hockey or table hockey—celebrate along with us.

Just like a game, we're dividing this modest chronicle into stages.

We'll begin with warmups, some relatively easy questions, and move along to the first, second, and third periods, with progressively tougher questions, and then shift to overtime and finally, a shootout, which will determine exactly how deep this river runs.

Along the way, we'll test your fandom and spin tales of the personalities involved in the answers, and skate the wing with some favorite things from nine decades of Blueshirts history.

Ready?

Drop the puck!

THE WARMUP

Okay, a bucket of pucks has been spilled onto our mythical fresh ice from the bench, and the starting goaltenders lead a line of players filtering from the corridor connected to the dressing room. The house lights brighten; the music is turned up.

Warmups are here: a choreographed 16-minute, pregame ritual of stretching, skating, passing, shooting, and sometimes, some brief schmoozing between former teammates (without crossing the red line, of course).

For you, it's a chance to loosen up with some easy questions.

1 Which teams did the Rangers eliminate in the playoffs on their thrilling climb to the Stanley Cup in the spring of 1994? And how many games did it take for each series to be decided? *Answer on page 5.*

2 How many sweater numbers are retired and hang from the rafters at Madison Square Garden? How many iconic players do they represent, and who's next? *Answer on page 7.*

3 How many times have the Rangers reached, if not won, the Stanley Cup Final? Bonus if you can name all the seasons and the results. *Answer on page 9.*

4 It's a tradition: Fans and the media in every city with NHL teams bestow nicknames on longtime or novelty trios. Match these 11 Rangers line combinations with their nicknames. *Answer on page 10.*

The Bread Line	Theo Fleury, Eric Lindros, Mike York
The Mafia Line	Ryan Hollweg, Dominic Moore, Jed Ortmeyer
The Czechmates	Walt Tkaczuk, Bill Fairbairn, Steve Vickers
The Bulldog Line	Rod Gilbert, Jean Ratelle, Vic Hadfield
The Fly Line	Jan Hlavac, Petr Nedved, Radek Dvorak
The Old Smoothies	Don Maloney, Phil Esposito, Don Murdoch
The HMO Line	Frank Boucher, Bill Cook, Frederick Joseph (Bun) Cook
The HBO Line	Rob McClanahan, Mark Pavelich, Anders Hedberg
The MPH Line	Bob Nevin, Phil Goyette, Donnie Marshall
The Battery Line	Brandon Dubinsky, Artem Anisimov, Ryan Callahan
The GAG Line	Ryan Hollweg, Blair Betts, Colton Orr

5 From Cablevision's James Dolan to New York Jets boss Sonny Werblin to Gulf & Western, the Rangers have had multiple owners—some controversial and most of them colorful. But who was the original owner of the franchise? *Answer on page 13.*

6 Each of the three top scorers in NHL history played part of their careers in New York. Name them and when they played at the Garden. *Answer on page 13.*

7 Eight Rangers have won the Calder Memorial Trophy as best rookie. Who was the only goaltender? Who are the others? *Answer on page 16.*

8 Speaking of trophies, how many Rangers have won the Vezina Trophy as top goaltender? Extra point: Who was the first hockey player to be featured on the cover of *Time Magazine*? *Answer on page 18.*

9 Emotions ran high on the night of October 7, 2001, the Rangers' regular-season home opener after the terrorist attacks that killed thousands and left part of downtown Manhattan in rubble. In the pregame ceremonies, first responders and police were honored and Mark Messier proudly wore a black fireman's helmet. What was the result in the first pro hockey game that counted in Manhattan after the attacks, and who scored the overtime goal? *Answer on page 20.*

10 Scoring 40 goals, in whatever year, is nothing to ignore. Nineteen Rangers have scored 40 or more in a season. Can you name half of them? *Answer on page 22.*

11 Of all the teams in franchise history, which compiled the most points in a regular season? *Answer on page 25.*

12 The current Madison Square Garden hosted the first Rangers game on February 18, 1968. Did the Blueshirts win? Who'd they play? *Answer on page 26.*

13 Consider this a heritage question. Match the marks with the record-holder. *Answer on page 27.*

Most Goals (career)	Harry Howell
Most Assists (career)	Bill Cook
Most Games Played (career)	Brian Leetch
Most 30-Goal Seasons (career)	Rod Gilbert
Most Penalty Minutes (career)	Mike Richter
Most Hat Tricks (career)	Emile Francis
Most Wins by a Coach (career)	Jean Ratelle
Longest Goal-Scoring Streak (season)	John Ross Roach
Most Saves (career)	Alain Vigneault
Most Shutouts (in a season)	Ron Greschner
Highest Points Percentage as a Coach (at least 100 game)	Andy Bathgate
Most Saves (game)	Henrik Lundqvist

14 One of the favorite fan awards is the annual Steven McDonald Extra Effort Award, presented at the end of every season since 1987–88 to the player who goes above and beyond the call of duty on and off the ice. The award was established to honor the police officer and devoted Rangers fan who was left a quadriplegic after being shot by a teenager while in the line of duty in Central Park. Six players have been selected twice or more. Who are they? *Answer on page 28.*

15 Who took over as starting goaltender when Mike Richter was forced to retire because of concussions in September 2002, and was the immediate predecessor to Henrik Lundqvist? *Answer on page 29.*

16 I called Cam Janssen "a meathead," David Clarkson "a bone-headed minor leaguer," goalie Martin Brodeur "a whiner and a big baby," and other opponents things not suitable for publication.

I wore Buddy Holly–style glasses in a photo for the media guide and an Elmer Fudd–like hunting jacket for a charity golf outing while my teammates wore collared knit shirts.

I interned for *Vogue Magazine*, dated actresses and models, and once sat with fans in the upper reaches of the Garden while recovering from injuries.

I'm _____. *Answer on page 30.*

THE WARMUP— ANSWERS

1 En route to their first sip from hockey's silver chalice in 54 years, the Rangers swept the Islanders, their eastern neighbors, in four games in the first round, then advanced to vanquish the Washington Capitals in five games.

In a classic Eastern Conference Final, it took seven games to oust the New Jersey Devils, the rivals across the Hudson River, and then another septet of games before dispatching the Vancouver Canucks, with the clincher coming on June 14 at Madison Square Garden.

It took 23 matches, with heroes galore, from established stars to players who would become household names in NHL lore.

The opening round wasn't even close: The Blueshirts torched the Islanders, outscoring them 22-3, with Mike Richter setting the tone by posting shutouts in the first two games. Alexei Kovalev scored in each game and the special-teams battle was no contest: The Rangers scored eight power-play goals in 27 opportunities; the Islanders were shut down, managing just one goal in 17 chances with the man-advantage.

The Capitals, with Jim Schoenfeld behind the bench, didn't put up much resistance either. At Madison Square Garden, the Rangers again took the first two games handily, 6-3 and 5-2, and Richter blanked Washington in the nation's capital in Game 3, 3-0, for the Rangers' seventh consecutive postseason victory. The Capitals avoided a sweep with a 4-2 win in the next game, but back at home, the Rangers ended any possibility of the visitors extending the second round when Brian Leetch netted the series-winner with 3:28 left in the third period for a 4-3 victory.

That set the stage for the dramatic, back-and-forth slugfest against the Devils, which featured three double-overtime games and following his "we'll win tonight" guarantee, Mark Messier's third-period hat trick in Game 6 to force a deciding Game 7.

The Devils took the opener in enemy territory, 4-3, on Stephane Richer's second-overtime goal, but the Rangers responded with a 4-0 whitewash at home. Another Stephane— Matteau—capped Game 3 at Meadowlands Arena with his first double-overtime score as Devils goalie Martin Brodeur faced 50 shots. It was the Devils' turn to respond, and they did, squaring the series at two games apiece with a 3-1 win and then marched into Madison Square Garden to take a 3-2 lead in the series with a 4-1 win in Game 5.

In one of the most clutch performances in playoff history, with the Rangers down 2-1 and on the brink of seeing their playoff run erased, Messier dominated the third period at the Meadowlands, scoring at 2:48, 12:12, and adding an empty-netter at 18:15 for a 4-2 triumph. In Game 7, it was Matteau scoring again in double-overtime for the memorable 2-1 win.

Give the Canucks credit. Down three games to one in the Final, they hung in with a victory in Game 5 at Madison Square Garden, exploding for five goals in the third period, and then a win in Game 6 at Pacific Coliseum, 4-1. Vancouver left wing Geoff Courtnall scored twice in each of those games.

So it came down to another Game 7 at the Garden during that indelible spring in New York. In the second period, another Messier power-play goal, with assists from Brian

Noonan and Adam Graves, proved to be the Cup winner in the 3-2 championship game.

2 Seven numbers—1, 2, 3, 7, 9, 11, and 35—are currently retired, representing eight players. Adam Graves and Andy Bathgate, who each wore No. 9, were honored in ceremonies on February 3 and February 22, 2009. In the 2017–18 season, center Jean Ratelle's No. 19 will be added, to bring the number to eight.

The first sweater to be raised was Rod Gilbert's No. 7, on October 14, 1979. In 15 seasons, Gilbert scored 406 goals and 1,021 points—both still stand as records—and was inducted into the Hall of Fame in 1982. A legitimate star from the mid-1960s to the late 1970s, the former right wing—and a player inexorably tied to Ratelle—remains a team ambassador and one of the most popular figures in franchise history.

The recognition of Ratelle, the lanky, smooth-skating center, is long overdue. Ratelle made his NHL debut and recorded his first career NHL goal and assist against the Maple Leafs in Toronto on March 4, 1961, and scored the final goal in the previous Madison Square Garden in a 3-3- tie with the Red Wings on February 11, 1968.

But 1971–72 was the most impressive season for Ratelle and Gilbert, longtime friends from Quebec, and Vic Hadfield. The three finished third, fourth, and fifth in scoring, with Ratelle collecting 109 points (46 goals and 63 assists) even though he broke his ankle with 16 games remaining in the season. He was named the NHL's MVP by his peers, winning the Lester B. Pearson Award, and with just two minor penalties all season captured the Lady Byng Trophy as the league's most gentlemanly player. He also was part of a blockbuster trade in

1975, when he was shipped to the Boston Bruins with defensemen Brad Park and Joe Zanussi for Phil Esposito and Carol Vadnais. Ratelle and Esposito are the only players who registered at least 400 points with both the Rangers and Bruins.

Here's a quick look at the other honorees, in chronological order.

Ed Giacomin's No. 1 was retired on March 15, 1989, two years after he was inducted into the Hall of Fame, and was at or near the top of the franchise's goaltending records when he left in 1975.

There were no other ceremonies until February 4, 2004, when Mike Richter's No. 35 took its place near the roof. Richter, a former Olympian, was the first American to be so honored.

Mark Messier's No. 11 joined the others on January 12, 2006. The iconic center, renowned for his leadership and six Stanley Cups, is the only player to ever captain two championship teams, the Rangers and Edmonton Oilers. His list of accomplishments is too lengthy to be recounted here.

Brian Leetch's No. 2 was the first Rangers defenseman's number to be retired, on January 24, 2008. Leetch rewrote every offensive record for a blueliner, and only Gilbert is ahead of him on the all-time scoring list.

Graves's exploits on the ice are matched only by his community service. The rugged winger was a two-time team MVP (1993, 1994). Bathgate led the team in scoring eight times from 1955 to 1963 and won the Hart Trophy as NHL MVP in 1958–59. A former captain, he was tied in points for the league scoring title in the 1961–62 season, but lost the Art Ross Trophy to Chicago's Bobby Hull because he had fewer goals.

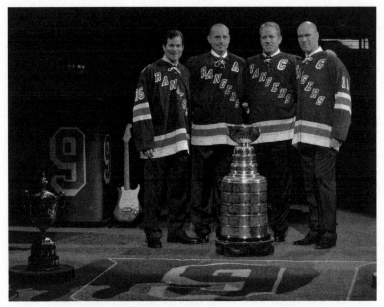

These members of the 1994 Stanley Cup–winning team—Mike Richter (35), Adam Graves (9), Brian Leetch (2), and Mark Messier (11)—wore four of the seven numbers retired as of the 2016–17 season. Graves was honored on February 3, 2009, at Madison Square Garden. (AP Photo/Kathy Willens)

Harry Howell, whose No. 3 was honored on February 22, 2009, played 17 years for the Rangers and 21 in the NHL and won the Norris Trophy as the league's top defenseman in 1966–67. "I'm glad I won the award," the former captain joked, "because it's going to belong to Bobby [Orr] from now on." He was close: the Bruins defenseman won it for the next eight seasons.

3 The Blueshirts have reached the NHL's championship round 11 times, winning the famous trophy four times: In 1928,

1933, 1940, and 1994. They've faced Toronto three times and Boston, Detroit, and Montreal each twice.

Here's the list:

2014	Lost in five games to the Los Angeles Kings, 4-1
1994	Beat the Vancouver Canucks in seven games, 4-3
1979	Lost in five games to the Montreal Canadiens, 4-1
1972	Lost in six games to the Boston Bruins, 4-2
1950	Lost in seven games to the Detroit Red Wings, 4-3
1940	Beat the Toronto Maple Leafs in six games, 4-2
1937	Lost to Detroit in five games, 3-2
1933	Beat the Toronto Maple Leafs in four games, 3-1
1932	Swept by Toronto in three games in a best-of-five series
1929	Lost to the Bruins 2-0 in a best-of-three series
1928	Beat the Montreal Maroons 3-2 in a best-of-five series

4 The Bread Line: Frank Boucher, Bill Cook, Frederick Joseph (Bun) Cook.

Boucher and the Cook brothers skated in the late 1920s and early 1930s, although the bakery reference was somewhat of a misnomer. A reporter noted that Fred, who is credited with creating the drop pass—leaving the puck for a trailing forward—was "quick as a bunny." "Bunny" was then shortened to "Bun."

The Mafia Line: Don Maloney, Phil Esposito, Don Murdoch.

The Italian reference to this line, which peaked in 1979, is to "A godfather and two dons."

The Czechmates: Jan Hlavac, Petr Nedved, Radek Dvorak.

These three natives of the European country lit the lamp regularly in 2000 and 2001.

The Bulldog Line: Bill Fairbairn, Walt Tkaczuk, Steve Vickers.

This gritty trio of the early '70s complemented the GAG line. Dave Balon was the right wing initially, but supplanted by Vickers. The center was Tkaczuk, of course. At first, fans pronounced his name "Tay-chuck" before they were corrected—it was "Ka-chook." A tenacious pivot who grew up in Canada but was born in Germany, he played 13 seasons on Broadway, and was so talented that he was able to change his game in mid-stream. In his first two full seasons, Tkaczuk led the team in scoring and was also a formidable two-way player, often killing penalties with Fairbairn. In the 1972 Stanley Cup Final against the Bruins, he shadowed and stifled Phil Esposito, and held him without a goal in six games. When an eye injury ended his career at age 33, he was fifth all time in games played with 945, sixth in points (678), 11th in goals with 227, and fifth in assists with 451.

The Fly Line: Theo Fleury, Eric Lindros, Mike York.

These speedsters led the team in scoring in 2002.

The Old Smoothies: Bob Nevin, Phil Goyette, Donnie Marshall.

These versatile veterans, acquired in trades from other clubs, helped the Blueshirts grab a playoff berth in 1966–67 for the first time in four years. Marshall and Goyette arrived from Montreal in 1963, and Nevin from Toronto in 1964.

The HMO Line: Ryan Hollweg, Dominic Moore, Jed Ortmeyer.

This high-energy, "in-your-face" fourth line, as termed by coach Tom Renney, played in 2005–06.

The HBO Line: Ryan Hollweg, Blair Betts, Colton Orr.

Betts replaced Dom Moore, who was traded, and enforcer Orr was acquired, and Coach John Tortorella put them together in 2007. Home Box Office was a very popular cable channel, so joining these initials as a successor to the HMO line was a no-brainer.

The MPH Line: Rob McClanahan, Mark Pavelich, Anders Hedberg.

More initials, and miles per hour, as well. Could've been called two Yanks and a Swede. They were a blur in 1982–83.

The Battery Line: Brandon Dubinsky, Artem Anisimov, Ryan Callahan.

This line, in place from 2010–2012, was christened for their energy, and also for the players' initials, which refer to battery sizes: D-AA-C.

The GAG Line: Rod Gilbert, Jean Ratelle, Vic Hadfield.

This threesome was for a stretch in the early 1970s the most productive line in team history, hence the "Goal-A-Game" abbreviation. They also sometimes were called the TAG Line ("Two-Goals-A-Game").

The GAG line was undoubtedly the one with the most electricity when it game to goals.

Ratelle was the ultimate playmaker; Hadfield was the captain and a physical presence; and Gilbert was the sniper. He had 12 seasons with 20 or more goals. At a game in Montreal, his hometown, on February 24, 1968, he fired so much rubber at the net (16 shots on goal) that it remains a team record.

Ratelle and Gilbert were friends since childhood, and the well-known tale is that Gilbert recommended Ratelle to scouts. What is lesser known is that Andy Bathgate was Gilbert's favorite player.

"Andy set the bar for what it means to be a Ranger," said Gilbert. "He was a true innovator of the game and my idol. As a young player, I was fortunate to have the opportunity to play with him and learn from him. He was class personified, on and off the ice."

That Gilbert had a pro career that lasted 18 years is stunning, given the fact that he had major back surgery and two spinal fusions.

5 The founder of the Rangers, George Lewis Rickard, was a former Texas cowboy, Alaska gold-rush pioneer of the late 1890s, saloon owner, and boxing promoter in Nevada, a sort of P.T. Barnum, who landed the rights to promote live events from Madison Square Garden and assembled the financing to build the new Garden, which was completed in 1925 on Eighth Avenue between 49th and 50th streets at a cost of $4.75 million.

Rickard forged a partnership with boxer Jack Dempsey and once told Dempsey: "Most folks are willing to believe anything you tell 'em. It's all about how it is presented. You gotta sell them good kid . . . let 'em think they got the best end of the deal."

The NHL awarded him a franchise for the 1926–27 season. One issue: The New York Americans had started playing at the Garden the previous season. That didn't stop Rickard, and the new team was quickly nicknamed "Tex's Rangers." Conn Smythe helped assemble that first team, which won the Stanley Cup in its second year. Smythe was fired before the first regular-season game, and replaced by Lester Patrick. Smythe moved on to become general manager of the Maple Leafs, and Toronto won six Stanley Cups between 1942 and 1951. Rickard died in 1929.

6 Wayne Gretzky, Jaromir Jagr, and Mark Messier.

Gretzky played three seasons in Manhattan: 1996–97 to 1998–99 before he retired. In all, the Great One, whose No. 99

was retired by the league in 2000, played 1,487 games and collected 894 goals and 2,857 points. As a Ranger, Gretzky notched 249 of those points—in just 234 games. He scored 57 goals and added 192 assists.

The Rangers only made it to the playoffs in his first season, however, and lost to the Philadelphia Flyers in the Eastern Conference Finals in five games.

Jagr, a powerful right wing, was 32 when he arrived in Manhattan in a trade with Washington for Anson Carter on January 20, 2004, played 31 games, then all 82 for the next three seasons.

The Czech legend, now 45, passed Messier for career points (1,888) in December 2016. Three hundred nineteen of those points came with the Rangers from 2004–2008. He had 124 goals and 195 assists in 277 games.

His finest year was 2005–06, when he set the franchise record for goals, points, and power-play goals in a season with 54, 123, and 24 respectively. Jagr also holds the individual season record for shots on goal (368).

Messier was a Ranger twice, from 1991–97 and 2000–04, and the most successful of the three players, leading the team to their first Cup since 1940 in 1994. On the brink of elimination in the Eastern Conference Finals, the captain confidently declared that the Blueshirts would win Game 6, and scored a natural hat trick in the third period, setting the stage for the seventh game, a double-overtime thriller that lifted the club to the Stanley Cup Final. He capped that off by scoring the winner in Game 7 against the Vancouver Canucks.

Of Messier's 1,887 points, more than a third (691) came wearing a Rangers sweater. He averaged almost a point per game: 250 goals and 441 assists in 698 regular-season games.

Holding his son Douglas, Mark Messier, who scored 691 points in 698 regular-season games as a Ranger and led the Blueshirts to their first Stanley Cup championship in 54 years in 1994, watches his No. 11 being raised to the rafters on Jan. 12, 2006, at Madison Square Garden. (AP Photo/ Frank Franklin II)

7 Lorne "Gump" Worsley was named the league's top rookie in 1952–53 at age 23. His record wasn't jaw-dropping—13-29-8, with a 3.06 goals against average. But the Rangers were dreadful that season, finishing dead last in the six-team league at 17-37-16.

Worsley was a character, in some ways, the Yogi Berra of the NHL.

Once asked, "Which team gives you the most trouble?," he replied, "The New York Rangers."

Rangers' coach Phil Watson once derided Worsley for having a beer belly. The response? "Just goes to show you what he knows. I only drink Johnnie Walker Red."

In 1961, a shot by Bobby Hull, considered the player with the hardest shot in the NHL, hit Worsley in the forehead, knocking him unconscious. When he awoke in the hospital, the Gumper said: "Good thing the puck hit me flat."

On a serious note, Worsley, who played 10 seasons with the Rangers before being shipped to Montreal in a trade for Jacques Plante, was a co-winner of the Vezina Trophy twice with the Canadiens, in 1965–66 (with Charlie Hodge) and 1967–68 (with Rogie Vachon).

The rest of the Calder winners? Several notables but also some lesser-knowns, for sure.

Kilby MacDonald, a former miner in Ontario, was 25 when he was selected during the 1939–40 Stanley Cup championship season, when the left wing scored 15 goals and 28 points in 44 games. MacDonald played 47 games in 1940–41 before serving a military stint. He returned to the Rangers in 1943 and ended up playing 151 regular-season games, scoring 36 goals and 70 points. In 15 playoff games, he had a goal and two assists for three points.

Grant "Knobby" Warwick was a 20-year-old right wing from Saskatchewan who scored 16 goals and 33 points in 44 games in 1941–42. He played almost seven seasons, scoring 17 or more goals in five of the next six with the Blueshirts before being traded to Boston.

Edgar Laprade, a smallish center, won the award in the 1945–46 season at age 26, with 15 goals and 34 points. The following season, he was selected for the inaugural NHL All-Star Game, the first of four for him. He played three full seasons without a penalty and won the Lady Byng Trophy in 1949–50.

Pentti Lund, who won the trophy in 1948–49, became the first Finnish-born player to score a goal in the NHL when the 23-year-old right wing scored 14 goals and 30 points in 59 games. He scored 18 goals the following season, and in the 1950 playoff run, which ended in a Stanley Cup Final loss to the Red Wings, he scored 11 points in 12 games.

Camille "The Eel" Henry was given the award in 1953–54 at age 21, when he went 24-15-39, edging the great Jean Beliveau. He won the Lady Byng in 1958, with only two minutes in penalties, and captained the team in 1964–65.

The Quebec City native was 5-foot-9 and about 150 pounds worth of elusiveness, the smallest player in the NHL in the late 1950s, with a talent for finding openings to redirect and tip shots past goaltenders, especially on the power play.

On November 1, 1959, when Jacques Plante first donned a mask, Henry scored the only goal against him and 255 more as a Ranger. His most was 37 goals in 60 games in the 1962–63 season.

He was traded to the Blackhawks in February 1965 for Doug Robinson, John Brenneman, and Wayne Hillman, but was brought back in 1967. Sometimes he took a beating from bigger defensemen and later wore knee braces. In 12 years, he was whistled for only 78 minutes in penalties.

The most recent Calder winners are much more familiar: Steve Vickers scored 30 goals and 53 points at age 21 in 1972–73 and 20-year-old Brian Leetch foreshadowed a magnificent career by winning the trophy in 1988–89 with 23 goals and 48 assists.

8 Five netminders who played on Broadway have won the Vezina.

They are:

Dave Kerr, 1939–40

Ed Giacomin and Gilles Villemure, 1970–71

John Vanbiesbrouck, 1985–86

Henrik Lundqvist, 2011–12

Kerr, an agile, athletic goalie with an impressive right glove hand who was 30 at the time, went 27-11-10 with a 1.54 goals-against-average and an NHL-best eight shutouts. Save percentage was not calculated until 1983–84, but the better goals-against-averages were below 2.00 at the time. The Toronto native was 8-4 with a 1.56 goals-against-average and three shutouts in the playoffs, when the Rangers knocked off both the Boston Bruins and the Maple Leafs in six games each to win the Cup.

His overall numbers with the Rangers: 157-110-57 from 1934–35 to 1940–41, with a 2.07 GAA and 40 shutouts. In the playoffs, he was 17-13-3, with a 1.57 GAA and seven shutouts.

Kerr is certainly the answer to another trivia question: Who was the first hockey player to be featured on the cover of *Time Magazine*? Kerr was on the March 14th, 1938, edition. In addition, of the five Vezina winners, he is the only one to win the Stanley Cup.

* * *

From 1964–65 through the 1980–81 season, goaltenders on the same team shared the trophy 12 times.

So it was not unusual when Giacomin (27-10-7, 2.16 GAA) and Villemure (22-8-4, 2.30), who split the duties in the crease, were named.

Vanbiesbrouck is the youngest of the recipients. At 22, he was 31-21-5 with a 3.32 GAA and .887 save percentage in 1985–86.

Lundqvist, who holds the majority of team records for a goaltender, is missing one significant accomplishment. He has won the Vezina, a gold medal in the Olympics, but not the ultimate prize, the Cup.

The Swede, who was drafted in the 7th round in 2000, leads the franchise in just about every key goaltending category: saves, save percentage, wins, playoff appearances (128—including 25 in a single season), and playoff wins (61). He is tied in playoff shutouts (10).

Lundqvist does not lead in single-season playoff records. Mike Richter had 16 wins in 1993–94, whereas Lundqvist had 13 in the 2013–14 postseason run before the loss to the Los Angeles Kings in the Final. Richter and Kerr also had four shutouts, and Lundqvist had three in 2011–12.

Among Rangers keepers who won Cups, Richter, who guarded the net in 1993–94 when Dominik Hasek won the Vezina, is about the closest to Lundqvist in many categories—second in wins (301), appearances (666), and saves (17,379).

In 1928, the goalie was Lorne Chabot, who was 41-25-14, with a 1.61 GAA and 21 shutouts in 80 games. But he was just 2-2-1 in the playoffs with a 1.50 GAA and two shutouts.

In 1933, Andy Aitkenhead was the keeper and was 6-1-1 with 1.48 GAA and two shutouts in the playoffs. Overall he was 47-43-16, with a 2.35 GGA and 11 shutouts.

9 Brian Leetch's tally, with assists from Petr Nedved and Zdeno Ciger at 2:45 of the extra session, defeated the Buffalo Sabres 5-4.

Leetch, of course, was a magnificent offensive defenseman, the best in the team's history. Born in Corpus Christi, Texas, but raised in Connecticut, Leetch also ranks as one of the top American blueliners ever and won a silver medal with Team USA in the 2002 Winter Olympics.

Leetch—undoubtedly the most valuable first-round draft pick in the franchise's 90-year history (ninth overall in 1986)—exploded on the scene at age 20 in 1988–89, scoring 23 goals and 48 assists in 68 games and capturing the Calder Trophy. He outdistanced 18-year-old Trevor Linden, who scored 30 goals for Vancouver, Quebec's Joe Sakic, and teammate Tony Granato.

In the 1991–92 season, Leetch was voted the NHL's top defenseman and took home the Norris Trophy. There was incredibly tough competition that season: Ray Bourque, Phil Housley, Scott Stevens, Larry Murphy, Chris Chelios were all in the running, but Leetch, just 23, garnered 65 of the 69 first-place votes. No wonder: He racked up 80 assists, just behind Los Angeles's Wayne Gretzky and Penguins center Mario Lemieux, and 102 points in 80 games.

When the Rangers won their first Stanley Cup in 54 years in 1994, Leetch played a critical role. He amassed 11 goals and 23 assists in 23 postseason games to be named playoff MVP, and thus awarded the Conn Smythe Trophy. He was the first

US-born winner and only the fifth defenseman to receive the recognition since its inception in 1965. The others were Montreal's Serge Savard (1969), Orr (1970, 1972), Montreal's Larry Robinson (1978), and Calgary's Al MacInnis (1989).

Numbers don't always tell the story of an athlete, but in Leetch's case, they are formidable.

In 17 years with the Rangers—before a much-maligned trade to the Maple Leafs near the end of the 2003–04 season for prospects Maxim Kondratiev and Jarkko Immonen, plus a first-round pick in the 2004 draft (which became Kris Chucko), and a second-round pick in 2005 (which became Michael Sauer)—Leetch scored 240 goals and added 741 assists in 1,129 games.

Those 741 assists, by the way, are the most in franchise history, and only Rod Gilbert is ahead of him on the all-time scoring list. Leetch ranks 8th on the all-time scoring list of defensemen and holds the all-time Rangers scoring streak of 17 games (five goals and 24 assists from November 23 to December 31, 1991). Leetch also collected 89 points in 82 playoff games to lead the all-time list.

Only two of the tens of thousands of NHL players won each of the following: the Calder Memorial Trophy, the James Norris Memorial Trophy, the Conn Smythe Trophy, and the Stanley Cup. The Blueshirt on the surprisingly short list is Leetch. The other is Boston legend Bobby Orr.

During a ceremony to retire his No. 2 in January 2008, Mark Messier, who Leetch succeeded as captain, called the defenseman "the greatest Ranger of all-time." On that night, Yankee Derek Jeter appeared on a video that concluded with the iconic shortstop saying: "So congratulations, from one number 2 to another." A year later, Leetch was inducted into the Hockey Hall of Fame.

Leetch's goal that October night ended the game and provided some closure, but some forget that the Rangers and Devils also met on September 19 at The Garden. Fans waved little American flags, players wore NYPD and FDNY stickers on helmets, and John Amirante sang "God Bless America." Advertising was removed from the boards and replaced with this: "Our thoughts and prayers are with the families of all the injured and lost, New York's Finest and Bravest, and all volunteers."

10 The names are certainly familiar, and it shouldn't come as any surprise that no defensemen are included. Seven are centers, seven are right wings, and five are left wings. Mike Gartner did it three times and Marian Gaborik and Jean Ratelle twice. The toughest to recall are probably Pat Hickey, Walt Poddubny, and John Ogrodnick.

Here's the list:

40 C Pat Hickey (1977–78); RW Tomas Sandstrom (1986–87); C Ron Duguay (1981–82); RW Mike Gartner (1991–92); LW Walt Poddubny (1986–87); RW Andy Bathgate (1958–59)

41 RW Marian Gaborik (2011–12); RW Pat Verbeek (1995–96); LW Steve Vickers (1974–75); C Jean Ratelle (1972–73)

42 C Phil Esposito (1978–79); RW Marian Gaborik (2009–10); LW Rick Nash (2014–15)

43 LW John Ogrodnick (1989–90); RW Rod Gilbert (1971–72)

45 RW Mike Gartner (1992–93)

46 C Jean Ratelle (1971–72)

47 C Mark Messier (1995–96)

48 C Pierre Larouche (1983–84)

49 RW Mike Gartner (1990–91)

50 LW Vic Hadfield (1971–72)

52 LW Adam Graves (1993–94)

54 RW Jaromir Jagr (2005–06)

Jaromir Jagr, the highest-scoring European player in NHL history, follows through after scoring his 54th goal of the season in Pittsburgh on April 13, 2006. The goal, backhanded past Penguins goalie Marc-Andre Fleury, set the Rangers' all-time goal-scoring record for a season. (AP Photo/Keith Srakocic)

Hickey was drafted in 1973 by two teams—the Rangers and that summer, the World Hockey Association's Toronto Toros—but rather than start in the NHL minors, he chose to learn from players like Bobby Hull and Frank Mahovlich in the high-flying WHA. Two years later, the speedy Hickey, notable for his flowing blond locks, came to New York, and his versatility—he could play either wing and center—made him a valuable tenth forward, filling in when one of the top nine was injured.

When he scored 40 goals, he was voted by fans as the most popular player on the team. He also scored 10 goals for Team Canada in the World Championships, including the winning goal in the bronze medal game. In 1985, after a few other NHL stops, he switched to the world of finance and also became an AHL executive.

Poddubny, who was raised near Thunder Bay, Ontario, where the Staal family—whose NHL-playing sons Marc, Eric, and Jordan all later grew up—was a true outdoorsman: he loved fishing, barbecue, and even dabbled in bear wrestling.

He came to the Rangers from the Maple Leafs in 1985. Knee problems after his rookie season, when he scored 59 points in 72 games, slowed him for much of the next two seasons, and he declined a second conditioning stint. The Leafs then traded him to the Blueshirts for Mike Allison.

His response? 40 goals and 47 assists in 75 games.

But his knees never recovered enough to reclaim those heights; his numbers declined, and Poddubny bounced around the NHL and Germany and later coached in the minor leagues. His life ended at age forty-nine when he collapsed at his sister's home.

Another member of this elite group, Ogrodnick could score, for sure. His 43-goal season in 1989–90 wasn't his best.

He had netted 55 in 1985—fourth in the NHL behind stars Wayne Gretzky, Jari Kurri, and Mike Bossy—with the Red Wings, with whom he played for seven and a half seasons. He also scored 41, 42, and 38 goals during his career, often playing with center Steve Yzerman.

The five-time All-Star with the exceptionally quick, accurate release, then twenty-eight, was sent to Quebec and then on October 1, 1987, to the Rangers, where a former teammate when he hit the double-nickel, Ron Duguay, was playing.

Rangers general manager Phil Esposito was concerned that the left winger was being wooed by the Penguins brass, who envisioned him on a line with playmaker extraordinaire Mario Lemieux. "Ogrodnick beside Lemieux in Pittsburgh would have 55 or 60 goals," said Esposito. "So forget it. I'd rather have him shooting for me than at me."

With linemates Kelly Kisio and Brian Mullen, Ogrodnick, whose forte was finding holes in the offensive zone and anticipating rebounds, shot as much as possible. More often than not, he hit the net.

11 The 2014–15 edition of the Blueshirts amassed 113 points and won the President's Trophy. The 1993–94 Cup-winning team collected 112. The next closest were three squads: 2011–12, 1970–71, and 1971–72, each with 109.

In five other years, the Rangers reached or surpassed 100:

1991–92 105
1972–73 102
2016–17 102
2015–16 101
2005–06 100

It should be duly noted that the points around the NHL tend to be higher after 2005, when the NHL eliminated ties, and teams received two points for an overtime or shootout win.

12 Before a crowd of 17,250 at the new building, sitting under the distinctively paneled, circular roof, the Rangers defeated the Philadelphia Flyers, 3-1.

The Blueshirts were third in the six-team East Division with a record of 27-18-11; the Flyers, in their first season as an expansion team, led the West at 25-23-8. The teams had split the first two games at the Spectrum in Philadelphia.

Typical of the games to come between the two rivals during the ensuing decades, there was a fight and seven penalties in the first period. Flyers goalie Doug Favell and rugged Ranger Reggie Fleming exchanged high sticks and then scrapped at 8:29 and each received major and minor penalties. Three other players also were sent to the box in the first 20 minutes: Flyers Ed Van Impe and Joe Watson and Rangers defenseman Jim Neilson.

But the teams were at even strength when the Flyers took a 1-0 lead. Wayne Hicks beat Eddie Giacomin at 12:12, with assists from captain Lou Angotti and Bill Sutherland.

The Rangers responded with three consecutive goals in the second period. Captain Bob Nevin scored the first Rangers goal at the new Garden, his 18th of the season, on an assist from Phil Goyette at 4:20, Donnie Marshall gave the Blueshirts the lead on a power play at 12:18 with assists from Nevin and Bernie "Boom-Boom" Geoffrion (who would later move behind the bench that season to coach), and Orland Kurtenbach finished the scoring at 17:27 on a helper from Rod Seiling. In the end, the Rangers outshot the Flyers 45-18.

Among the other Rangers in the lineup that day: Wayne Hillman, Harry Howell, Arnie Brown, Rod Gilbert, Vic Hadfield, Jean Ratelle, Larry Jeffrey, and Ron Stewart. The team lost to the Canadiens 7-2 three days later at the new arena.

In that inaugural 1967–68 season, Walt Tkaczuk played his first game as a Ranger, and Gilbert and Ratelle finished fourth and fifth in the NHL in scoring behind Stan Mikita, Phil Esposito, and Gordie Howe.

The Rangers finished second in the East, but lost to the Chicago Blackhawks in six games in the Eastern Conference Quarterfinals. The Flyers ended atop the Western Conference, ahead of the five other expansion teams—the Los Angeles Kings, St. Louis Blues, Minnesota North Stars, Pittsburgh Penguins, and Oakland Seals—but fell to the Blues in seven games in the first round of the playoffs.

13 If you were paying attention above, there are some gimmes here: Harry Howell played the most games in blue (1,160), Rod Gilbert has the most goals (406), and Brian Leetch has the most assists (741).

But did you figure out the trickier ones?

Bill Cook had the greatest number of hat tricks (11), Ron Greschner was in the penalty box the most (1,226 minutes), and Henrik Lundqvist has had 22,810 saves. But Richter made the most saves in a game, with 59, in Vancouver on January 31, 1991, a 3-3 tie. John Ross Roach had the most shutouts, 13 in 1928–29. Emile Francis has the most wins as a coach with 342, but Alain Vigneault had the higher points percentage, .628 (at the end of the 2016–17 season). Jean Ratelle, with six, had the most 30-goal seasons. The longest goal-scoring streak belongs to Andy Bathgate: Ten games, with 11 total goals, from December 15, 1962, to January 5, 1963.

Most Assists	Brian Leetch
Most Games Played	Harry Howell
Most 30-Goal Seasons	Jean Ratelle
Most Penalty Minutes	Ron Greschner
Most Hat Tricks	Bill Cook
Most Wins by a Coach	Emile Francis
Longest Goal-Scoring Streak	Andy Bathgate
Most Saves	Henrik Lundqvist
Most Shutouts in a Season	John Ross Roach
Most Goals	Rod Gilbert
Most Saves (game)	Mike Richter
Highest Points Percentage	Alain Vigneault

14 Presented at the end of each regular season on ice at Madison Square Garden, two players have dominated the voting: Adam Graves won five times (in the spring of 1992, 1993, 1994, 1999, 2000) and Ryan Callahan four times (2009, 2010, 2012, 2013).

But Mats Zuccarello is a close third (2014, 2016, 2017).

Mark Messier (1995, 1996), Sandy McCarthy (2001, 2002), Jed Ortmeyer (2004, 2007), and Jan Erixon, who also was the first recipient in 1988 and again in 1991, all won twice.

The most emotional and heart-wrenching of all the ceremonies happened during the Spring of 2017, before the regular-season finale against the Penguins. It was the first after the passing of McDonald, 59, a bastion of determination, humor, and grace, from a heart attack in January.

On the ice at the Garden, his widow, Patti Ann, wiped away tears and rested her head on the shoulder of her son,

Conor, now a detective himself and wearing dress blues. During a video tribute from Rangers players, Zuccarello said, "We will never forget him." When Zuccarello's name was announced, he skated from the bench to the family and warmly embraced Patti Ann and Conor.

"I met him a few times outside [the Garden], so I know them a little bit," he said. "So I just thought that he's here with us and stay strong. It was an emotional moment for them and emotional for me."

The ceremony was particularly touching for Zuccarello who, just two years before, was hospitalized with a skull fracture and bleeding on the brain after a slap shot hit him in the left side of the head during Game 5 of the playoffs against the Penguins. He lost the ability to speak for four days, and was deeply concerned that his career was over. But after a summer of therapy, Zuccarello slowly recovered and showed up for training camp the following fall.

In remarks reminiscent of his father's annual comments from his wheelchair, Conor, 30, urged the Rangers to "go above and beyond" in the Stanley Cup playoffs. "Our greatest memories were in this Garden as Ranger fans," he said. "It's not supposed to be easy, but I'm telling the boys in blue to get the job done."

From the stands, there were tears and cheers for the hero who had forgiven the teenager who shot him. "It was really hard not having Steven there," his widow said, "but we could feel the hug from everyone at the Garden tonight."

15 Mike Dunham, one of the few players to dress for all three New York metropolitan-area teams, was the tweener. Dunham, who started his NHL career with the Devils and was a third-round draft pick (53rd overall in 1990), won the William M. Jennings Trophy with Martin Brodeur for the lowest team goals against average in the 1996–97 season.

Dunham was selected by Nashville in the expansion draft and after four seasons was traded to New York for Tomas Kloucek, Rem Murray, and the rights to Marek Zidlicky in December 2002.

He played 100 games for the Blueshirts over two seasons, 43 in 2002–03, and finished 19-17-5, with a 2.29 GAA and a solid .924 save percentage. He also won a silver medal in the 2002 Winter Olympics with the US team.

At 31, he slipped a bit in 2003–04, when, in 57 games, he was 16-30-6 with a 3.03 GAA and .896 save percentage. To be fair, the Rangers were horrible that season, winning just 27 games, and used four other goalies: Jussi Markkanen, Jamie McLennan, Jason LaBarbera, and Steve Valiquette.

16 Love him or hate him, Sean Avery didn't hold much back, on or off the ice. That's why he was known as an agitator deluxe.

During two seasons in Los Angeles, he was fined by the Kings, suspended, accused of racial slurs, and eventually traded to the Blueshirts on February 6th, 2007, for Jason Ward, Marc-Andre cliché, and Jan Marek.

The 5-foot-10 winger from Pickering, Ontario was overwhelmingly named as the most hated skater in a players' poll in *The Hockey News*, collecting more than 66 percent of the vote, and also was fingered as the most over-rated. That's not how the Garden Faithful saw it.

For them, he was a sparkplug, adding some energy and snarl.

In his first 18 games as a Blueshirt, Avery scored three goals and nine points, and the Rangers made the playoffs. The following season, on February 16, 2008, 10 seconds into a game against the Buffalo Sabres, he set the record for the fastest Rangers goal on home ice.

In the 2008 playoffs against the Devils, he faced Brodeur at the top of the crease, screening him by mimicking his movements and waving his stick and hands, which prompted the league to change the rules to prohibit such antics. That feud had been simmering since a February game in 2007, when the two exchanged shoves, and continued after the Rangers won the playoff series in five games. Brodeur avoided Avery on the ice post-game, and Avery shot back: "Fatso forgot to shake my hand."

Avery moved on to Dallas in 2008, agreeing to a four-year, $15.5 million contract that was never completed. The NHL suspended him for six games after comments about players dating some former girlfriends (he termed them "sloppy seconds") and the Stars waived him. Less than a month later, Rangers general manager Glen Sather offered him another chance, which lasted for parts of four seasons.

However, under no-nonsense bench boss John Tortorella, hired to replace Tom Renney on February 23, 2009, it was the beginning of the end for Avery on Broadway, where he had dabbled in modeling and investing in restaurants. The two simply didn't mesh. The Rangers missed the playoffs and matters went downhill. It didn't help that Avery then scored just three goals in 2010–11 in 76 games, and amassed 174 penalty minutes. Tensions increased and the following season, Avery played just 15 games, bouncing back and forth to the AHL. "I think we have better players than Sean Avery, plain and simple," Tortorella said.

In all, Avery played 264 games for the Rangers, amassing 601 penalty minutes, 45 goals, and 123 points. When he left the game in 2012, he announced his retirement on a Bravo television show and parted with this remark: "I threw my skates in the Hudson."

FIRST PERIOD

Well, those warmups weren't too challenging, were they? Good.

Jerseys changed? Laces tightened? Stick taped just so? Game-face on? We're ready for the first period.

Be ready to change on the fly, be challenged, checked, cheered, and booed.

Did you know that NHL teams that led after the first period won 590 games and lost only 115 in regulation during the 2015–16 season? So, ladies and gentlemen, try to get off to a good start . . .

1 Trades between the Rangers and Islanders have been few and far between. In fact, there have been just two. The last one took place in May 2010, when the Blueshirts acquired Jyri Niemi in exchange for a sixth-round pick in the 2010 draft. But who was the first former Ranger to wear an Islanders jersey? *Answer on page 39.*

2 When you are honored with an opportunity to skate with the best players in the NHL, you have to stand out. That's what five Rangers did when they were named MVP at NHL All-Star games. Who are they? *Answer on page 40.*

3 Here's a change-up. Multiple choice: How many players who wore the Rangers jersey are in the Hockey Hall of Fame?

a. 31   b. 39

c. 45   d. 51

e. 60

How many can you name? Who was the first and who was the most recent inductee? *Answer on page 42.*

4 In 1976, this Rangers forward set the single-game record for points in a game with seven. He was known as Sarge. Who is he? *Answer on page 45.*

5 Lars-Erik Sjoberg never played for the Rangers, but his legacy is honored every fall. How do the Blueshirts pay tribute to the former defenseman every year? *Answer on page 46.*

6 How many Hobey Baker Award winners, given annually to the top NCAA player since 1981, played for the Rangers? Who's the most recent? *Answer on page 50.*

7 We are considered the "Royal Family" of hockey for innovation, coaching, and championships and our bloodlines run through the Rangers. We are the _____. *Answer on page 52.*

8 Everyone recalls the indelible image of Mark Messier's joyous celebration after his goal to secure the 1994 Stanley Cup with a 3-2 win in Game 7. It was the only Cup that the Rangers have won in Madison Square Garden.

Three other players scored Cup-winning goals for the Rangers. Who are they? *Answer on page 54.*

9 Match this baker's dozen of former and current Rangers with their nickname. And if you know how they received the moniker, even better. Give yourself some extra points. *Answer on page 56.*

Andy Hebenton	Nifty
Rick Middleton	Murder
Alf Pike	Taffy
Erik Christensen	Boxcar
Ed Hospodar	The Crusher
Gilles Marotte	Captain Crunch
Don Murdoch	The Cat
Clarence Abel	Seldom
Emile Francis	Spuds
Mats Zuccarello	Goalbuster
Cam Talbot	Frodo
Frank Beaton	The Embalmer

10 Which Ranger rookie posted the most points as a freshman? And a few years after that, who netted the most goals as a rookie? *Answer on page 57.*

11 Over the years, the Rangers' minor-league affiliates have groomed players such as Bill Fairbairn, Alex Kovalev, Camille Henry, Brandon Dubinsky, and Derek Stepan for the Big Show. Their American Hockey League team has been in Hartford since 1997, but the club's top affiliate has been in 11 other locations since 1926. How many of them can you name? *Answer on page 60.*

12 He was a prankster, always ready with a quip, a steady center with 20-plus-goal seasons and who still provides some analysis of games on the radio. But what is Pete Stemkowski best known for? *Answer on page 62.*

13 Living in the media capital of the world, of course the Rangers would be invited to appear on David Letterman's late-night show. Different Rangers read "Top 10 Lists" twice, once in 1995 and again in 2009. And one defenseman fired some shots—and quips—at Letterman on the rink at Rockefeller Center in 1984. Can you name a few of the players who starred on the small screen? *Answer on page 64.*

14 Which Rangers coach leads in wins? Who's No. 2? And here's a true or false: Together, is it possible that ten coaches have more than twice as many wins as the remaining 24? *Answer on page 65.*

15 Who were the first Russian-born players ever to have their names engraved on the Stanley Cup? *Answer on page 67.*

16 How many Rangers belong to The Century Club— having scored 100 or more points in a season? *Answer on page 69.*

17 When was the only time an opposing goalie was robustly cheered from the opening faceoff to the end of the game? *Answer on page 69.*

18 When rivalries come up for debate, Rangers-Islanders, Rangers-Devils, and Rangers-Flyers are always among the top contenders for the best and bloodiest. But the earliest Blueshirts rivalry occurred when these two teams banged heads—and also played the longest game in any of the four Madison Square Gardens. Name the other club. *Answer on page 71.*

19 In 1979, the Rangers beat the Los Angeles Kings two straight in the first round of the playoffs, the Flyers in five games, and a six-game battle royale against the Islanders to reach the Stanley Cup Final against the Montreal Canadiens in 1979. What happened in warmups of Game 2 that turned the series around as the Canadiens rebounded to win in five? *Answer on page 72.*

20 The Lone Ranger, Pentti Lund, Don "Bones" Raleigh, Pete Babando, and the Ringling Bros. all played significant roles in the 1949–50 Stanley Cup playoff run, a near-miss for the Blueshirts, who pushed the Final to seven games. How did each of the above figure in the outcome? *Answer on page 73.*

FIRST PERIOD—
ANSWERS

1 The first trade between the two teams took place on November 14, 1972, as Rangers dealt right wing Ron Stewart to the expansion team for cash. He played 22 games for the Islanders that season with two goals and two assists.

But Blueshirts defenseman Arnie Brown, who started his career as a prospect with the Toronto Maple Leafs, was the first ex-Ranger to wear an Islanders sweater after a four-player deal with Detroit on October 4, 1972.

Brown, a defense-first defenseman, was acquired from Toronto by the Rangers in February 1964, along with four other players—Dick Duff, Bob Nevin, Rod Seiling, and Billy Collins—in exchange for Andy Bathgate and Don McKenney, and partnered with Harry Howell on Broadway.

After Howell, Brown was paired with Brad Park and transformed into a more offensive player, notching 36 points in 1969–70. During the playoffs that season, his knees gave way and required several operations, and was eventually sent to the Red Wings, who shipped him to the Islanders in October 1972. He played 48 games for the Isles that season, with four goals and 12 points.

There also was an Islander who played a significant role in one of their Stanley Cup–winning seasons who was a Ranger for less than a day.

Roland Melanson, called "Rollie the Goalie," had replaced Glenn (Chico) Resch in February 1981. He only played 11 games in 1980–81, because Billy Smith played 41 as Long Islanders celebrated a second Cup.

But during the 1982–1983 season, Melanson started 44 games, three more than Smith, and the duo shared the Jennings Trophy, awarded to teams with the lowest goals-against-average. He sat down in the playoffs, however, and the Isles beat the Edmonton Oilers for their fourth consecutive championship.

Fast forward to November 1984.

With young Kelly Hrudey waiting in the wings, Melanson was shipped to the Minnesota North Stars, where he stayed about three weeks. On December 9, 1984, the Rangers traded for Melanson, sending two draft picks to the North Stars, then immediately flipped him, along with Grant Ledyard, to the Los Angeles Kings for Brian McLellan and a fourth-round pick. Melanson never had a chance to pull on the Rangers sweater.

2 Don Maloney, Mike Gartner, Mike Richter, Wayne Gretzky, and Marian Gaborik.

In 1984, Don Maloney played for the Wales Conference, which edged the Campbell Conference in a 7-6 win. Maloney and fellow Ranger Pierre Larouche didn't have to travel far— the event was staged at the Meadowlands Arena in East Rutherford, New Jersey. Maloney had three assists through the second period, including one on Larouche's goal that made it 6-3, Wales. Maloney, who would finish that season with 24 goals and 66 points, scored the first goal of the third period.

* * *

Talk about an offensive explosion.

At the Montreal Forum in 1993, Mike Gartner became the fourth player to score four goals in one All-Star game during a Wales Conference rout, 16-6.

Gartner, who had been named as a replacement for Mark Messier and wore No. 11, made it easy for the MVP voters: He scored 3:15 into the game, again 22 seconds later, assisted on Peter Bondra's goal at 4:24, and completed a first-period hat trick at 13:22. His fourth goal came at 3:33 of the second period, for a quartet of goals and five points in just over 20 minutes.

The goals equaled the record set by Wayne Gretzky, Mario Lemieux, and Vincent Damphousse.

Gartner, who would lead the team in goals that year with 45, had also won the fastest skater race in the All-Star skills competition.

* * *

In 1994, on his home ice at Madison Square Garden, Richter was spectacular, stopping 19 of 21 shots in the second period, including three breakaways by Vancouver's Pavel Bure in the 9-8 win by the Eastern Conference.

In a flashback months later, Richter again denied Bure, this time on a memorable penalty shot in Game 4 of the Stanley Cup Final, which the Rangers won.

Sadly, injuries to his MCL, ACL, a fractured skull, and multiple concussions over several seasons ended the Flourtown, Pennsylvania, native's career far too soon. Richter finished with a record of 301-258-73 in 666 regular season games, with a 2.89 goals-against-average and a .904 save percentage, along with 24 shutouts. In the playoffs, he was 41-33, with a 2.68 GAA, a .909 save percentage, and nine shutouts.

In retrospect, the All-Star honor was just another accomplishment: He was a silver medalist in the 2002 Olympics and was in goal for the inaugural World Cup of Hockey in 1996 for Team USA and was named tournament MVP.

* * *

In his 18th and final All-Star Game in 1999, Gretzky, who captained the North American squad against the World All-Stars, won his third MVP for his performance at the Ice Palace in Tampa, Florida, as the Canadian-filled team won 8-6. Gretzky had a goal and two assists.

Gretzky's final NHL game would come later that season, a 2-1 overtime loss to the Pittsburgh Penguins. He scored his final point in this game, assisting on Brian Leetch's goal. Gretzky was named as the first, second, and third star. In the last campaign for No. 99, he scored nine goals and 62 points, but the Rangers would miss the playoffs that year.

* * *

In 2012, Marian Gaborik had a hat trick in Ottawa with two of the goals against then-teammate Henrik Lundqvist. The two had chirped all week after Zdeno Chara's team "drafted" Gaborik, while Daniel Alfredsson's team, with Lundqvist, had passed over the talented winger, who had already scored 25 goals. Alfredsson even picked Rangers defenseman Dan Girardi over Gaborik.

And when Gaborik, who also had an assist and won the MVP in the 12-9 victory, scored his second against The King, he celebrated with the knee-down, sniper pose that yet another Ranger—Artem Anisimov—had used. Gaborik had 41 goals and 76 points in his last full season with the Rangers before he was traded.

3 As of the Class of 2016, 51 men who played for the Rangers were inducted into the Hockey Hall of Fame. Howie Morentz was the first in 1945, and Eric Lindros was the last.

Best known as a Philadelphia Flyer, center Eric Lindros, who scored 66 goals and 158 points in 192 games as a Ranger, celebrates after teammate Mike York scored against the Sabres in Buffalo's HSBC Arena on November 10, 2001. Lindros was elected to the Hall of Fame in 2016. (AP Photo/Don Heupel)

The rest: Lester Patrick (1947), Bill Cook (1952), Frank Boucher (1958), Ching Johnson (1958), Earl Siebert (1963), Doug Bentley (1964), Babe Siebert (1964), Max Bentley (1966) Babe Pratt (1966), Neil Colville (1967), Bryan Hextall (1969), Bill Gadsby (1970), Terry Sawchuk (1971), Bernie Geoffrion (1972), Doug Harvey (1973), Chuck Rayner (1973), Art Coulter (1974), Johnny Bower (1976), Tim Horton (1977), Andy Bathgate (1978), Jacques Plante (1978), Harry Howell (1979), Harry Lumley (1980), Lynn Patrick (1980), Gump

Worsley (1980), Allan Stanley, (1980), Rod Gilbert (1982), Bobby Hull (1983), Phil Esposito (1984), Jean Ratelle (1985), Ed Giacomin (1987), Guy Lafleur (1988), Buddy O'Connor (1988), Brad Park (1988), Clint Smith (1991), Marcel Dionne (1992), Edgar Laprade (1993), Fred Bun Cook (1995), Wayne Gretzky (1999), Mike Gartner (2001), Jarri Kurri (2001), Pat LaFontaine (2003), Dick Duff (2006), Mark Messier (2007), Glenn Anderson (2008), Brian Leetch (2009), Luc Robataille (2009), Pavel Bure (2012), and Brendan Shanahan (2013).

Note: Only about a dozen of these players spent the majority of their careers as Rangers.

Many of the players, like Bill Gadsby for example, were short-time Rangers but had terrific backstories.

One of the least appreciated Rangers defensemen—perhaps because he was with the Blueshirts for just seven seasons—was Bill Gadsby. From 1954–55 to 1960–61, Gadsby was a five-time All-Star and voted the Rangers' most valuable player in 1955–56, when he set the league's single-season record for assists (42) and points (51) by a defenseman. The assist record stood until Boston's Bobby Orr smashed it in 1969–70, when he had 87.

Beyond hockey, his life story is remarkable. When Gadsby was only 12 years old, in September 1939, the *Athenia*, a ship on which he and his mother were travelling, was torpedoed and sunk by German U-boats off northwestern Ireland. One hundred twelve passengers and crew died, but the Gadsbys survived.

While in training camp with the Chicago Blackhawks in 1952, he contracted polio, but recovered. He was traded to the Rangers in 1954, and thrived.

In the 1958–59 season, the Calgary native finished just behind Montreal's Tom Johnston for the Norris Trophy as the

NHL's top defender. In those years, the Red Wings were always close to a championship, and Detroit finally acquired Gadsby on June 12, 1961, in exchange for Les Hunt.

He played 457 of his 1,248 games on Broadway.

After one year with the Wings, he almost retired, but hung in to chase the Cup. He came close three times, getting to the Final in 1963, 1964, and 1966, only to fall short. When he hung up the skates after that third loss, at age 34, he estimated that he had received about 600 stiches in his face during his career, and he retired as the highest scoring defenseman in NHL history.

Another nine former Rangers coaches or executives have been honored in the Builders category: John Kilpatrick, William Jennings, Emile Francis, Bud Poile, Glen Sather, Craig Patrick, Roger Neilson, Herb Brooks, and Fred Shero.

4 On February 18, 1976, Steve Vickers had a hat trick against Washington Capitals goalie Ron Low and four assists in an 11-4 rout at the Garden.

Vickers, who wore No. 8, was the Rangers' first-round pick in the 1971 amateur draft (10th overall) and established his on-ice office at the left post, where he was always ready to slam in a rebound, on his forehand or backhand.

He was 21 when the Rangers opened the 1972 season in Detroit. There was instant chemistry with Walt Tkaczuk and Billy Fairbairn, the trio which would be called "The Bulldog Line." Vickers scored on his first shot on goal. After Gene Carr, the original left wing with Tkaczuk and Fairbairn, broke his collarbone, Vickers was the spark again. He scored a hat trick against the Los Angeles Kings on November 12, and matched that against the Philadelphia Flyers in the next game. At the time, no one in NHL history had done that.

So after more than a dozen candidates had been tried on the left side of Tkaczuk to replace Dave Balon, who had been traded in 1971, the line was set. His back-to-back hat trick record didn't last very long, however. Vancouver's Bobby Schmautz scored three times and then followed it up with four the next game. Vickers exclaimed: "That's something . . . and he did it without Tkaczuk and Fairbairn!"

Vickers, who was pounded by defensemen trying to move him away from the net, also established a reputation for toughness, as well as scoring. Said Rangers scout/player personnel director Steve Brklacich: "He doesn't start fights, he finishes them." He was named rookie of the year after scoring 30 goals and 23 assists and contributed nine points in 10 playoff games. Because he wore an old Army jacket, Pete Stemkowski named him "Sarge."

As injuries mounted and coaching changes favored speed, Vickers spent less time on the power play and his production diminished. After being sent to Springfield, the team's American Hockey League affiliate in the 1981–82 season, he retired. Vickers scored 246 goals and 586 points, plus 24 goals and 49 points in the postseason. That is still enough for 8th place on the team's all-time scoring list.

5 Since 1988, Sjoberg, a talented defenseman who was born in Falun, Sweden, and was the chief European scout for the Rangers when he died of cancer at age 43, has been honored every year when the top rookie in training camp—as voted by the New York media—is given the Lars-Erik Sjoberg Award.

A speedy, compact blueliner, Sjoberg played for three teams—Leksands, Djurgardens, and Vastra Frolunda (where

Henrik Lundqvist would later thrive before coming to New York)—in that hockey-mad country for 12 years, from 1962 to 1974.

With Frolunda, he won the Golden Puck as Swedish player of the year in the 1968–69 season. That coveted award puts him among the luminaries who captured that honor, including Lundqvist (2004–05), Peter Forsberg (1992–93, 1993–94), Daniel and Henrik Sedin (1998–99), Henrik Zetterberg (2001–02), Kent Nilsson (1988–89), and Hakan Loob (1982–83). He played for the Swedish national team in the Winter Olympics in 1968 and 1972 and captained Sweden's national team in the 1976 Canada Cup.

Sjoberg's notoriety didn't waver when he came to North America. He was the first non–North American born-and-raised captain in the NHL, when he wore the "C" for the Winnipeg Jets during the 1979–80 season, the team's first in the league. At age 30, Sjoberg had signed as a free agent with Winnipeg in the World Hockey Association in 1974 and played for five seasons, scoring 25 goals and 194 points in 295 regular-season games. He was named the circuit's top defenseman in 1977–78, when he scored 11 goals and 50 points in 78 games.

For the Rangers, Sjoberg scouted players in Europe for eight years, and based on his recommendations, the team drafted players such as power forward Tomas Sandstrom, who would later win a Stanley Cup with the Detroit Red Wings; Jan Erixon, who played 10 years on Broadway; left wing Ulf Dahlen, who played 14 years in the NHL; and Kjell Samuelsson, the physical defenseman who won a Cup with the Pittsburgh Penguins in 1992 and played most of his career with the Philadelphia Flyers.

Here's the list of the players who have been presented with the Lars-Erik Sjoberg Award through 2016:

- 1988 Mike Richter
- 1989 Troy Mallette
- 1990 Steven Rice
- 1991 Tony Amonte
- 1992 Peter Andersson
- 1993 Mattias Norstrom
- 1994 Mattias Norstrom
- 1995 Niklas Sundstrom
- 1996 Eric Cairns
- 1997 Marc Savard
- 1998 Manny Malhotra
- 1999 Kim Johnsson
- 2000 Filip Novak
- 2001 Dan Blackburn
- 2002 Jamie Lundmark
- 2003 Dominic Moore
- 2005 Henrik Lundqvist
- 2006 Nigel Dawes and Brandon Dubinsky
- 2007 Marc Staal
- 2008 Lauri Korpikoski
- 2009 Matt Gilroy
- 2010 Derek Stepan
- 2011 Carl Hagelin
- 2013 Jesper Fast
- 2014 Anthony Duclair
- 2015 Oscar Lindberg
- 2016 Jimmy Vesey

As you can see, receiving the award doesn't guarantee a place in Rangers history. Recent honorees such as Carl Hagelin, Anthony Duclair (prematurely dubbed the "Duke of New York"), and Brandon Dubinsky were traded, and have earned accolades around the league. Steven Rice, dripping with potential, played 11 games before he was traded to Edmonton in the deal to bring Mark Messier to New York. Mattias Norstrom had a long career in Los Angeles.

Others never extended their NHL careers: Filip Novak, drafted 64th overall in 2000, never played for the Rangers. Peter Andersson, a defenseman, played just 39 games before spending the bulk of his career in Europe.

Another player who had the makings of a star but whose career never came to fruition was Dan Blackburn.

Drafted in 2001, the tenth player selected overall, the Ontario native was seen as the heir apparent to Mike Richter, and became the second youngest goalie in franchise history to appear in an NHL game (18 years, 143 days) on October 10, 2001.

When the Blueshirts beat Montreal five days later, Blackburn became the third youngest goaltender in NHL history—and second in franchise history—to record a win. He made 18 consecutive starts from November 7 to December 14, and backing up Richter, appeared in 31 games with a 12-16-0 record. By ending the 2002 season with five straight wins, Blackburn became just the second goalie under 19 to accomplish that (Buffalo's Tom Barrasso was the other).

Blackburn returned in 2002–03, but shared the crease with other goaltenders, because Richter suffered a concussion. He would play in 32 games, going a dismal 8-16-4.

That fall, Blackburn suffered nerve damage in his left shoulder, apparently from lifting weights, and missed the

2003–04 season. He couldn't rotate his shoulder to have his glove hand in the proper position to stop pucks. And the damage slowed his speed.

He had exploratory surgery, and gave what was a promising career one more shot.

While playing with the ECHL's Victoria Salmon Kings, Blackburn tried using two blockers instead of one.

With a normal blocker on his stick side, the one on his glove side was specially designed: The waffle faced the shooter; the underside of the odd-blocker was a modified catching glove. He could catch low shots and cover loose pucks with that side.

Yet Blackburn played only 12 games with Victoria, going 3-9-0. After tearing the MCL in his left knee, he retired. He was just 22.

6 Six played for the Blueshirts, but only three did so as their first NHL team out of college: George McPhee (Bowling Green, 1982), Matt Gilroy (Boston University, 2009), and Jimmy Vesey (Harvard), who was the most recent honoree, winning in 2016.

Chris Drury (Boston University, 1998), Mike Mottau (Boston College, 2000), and Jason Krog (New Hampshire, 1999) also played on Broadway.

* * *

In the 1982–83 season, McPhee played for the Central Hockey League's Tulsa Oilers, and joined the Rangers for nine playoff games and another nine regular-season games the following year. The Guelph, Ontario native skated for the Rangers for three consecutive seasons, from 1984–85 to 1986–87. A left wing, McPhee had 24 goals and 49 points in 115 games. In the 1983 playoffs, he and Ray Cote of the Edmonton Oilers became the first players to score three goals in a single post-season prior to playing a regular-season NHL game. McPhee later worked in the front offices of the Vancouver Canucks, the Washington Capitals, and in 2016, became the general manager of the Vegas Golden Knights.

Defenseman Matt Gilroy, who grew up on Long Island, signed a two-year, $3.5 million contract and played 69 games (4-11-15) in 2009–10 and 58 games in 2010–11 (3-8-11) and also spent time in the AHL. In 2012–13, he returned for 15 games and then played in Russia's KHL for several seasons.

Drury, who grew up in Connecticut, was the most successful player of the half-dozen and considered one of most clutch players in the NHL. With the Colorado Avalanche, he won a Calder Trophy in 1998–98 and a Stanley Cup in 2000–01, as well as two silver medals playing for the US in the Winter Olympics in 2002 and 2010. He also captained the Buffalo Sabres and the Rangers.

With the Rangers, Drury played the final three full seasons of his career before he retired in August 2011 at age 34. The Blueshirts made the playoffs all three seasons. In all, Drury, who is now the Rangers' assistant general manager, played 264 games in New York, with 62 goals and 151 points, and added four goals and eight points in 21 postseason games.

Vesey's career is just beginning. After being drafted by the Nashville Predators, he declined to sign and became a free agent in the summer of 2016. He agreed to a three-year contract with the Rangers after being hotly pursued by almost a dozen teams. Vesey had 16 goals and 11 assists in his rookie season and was 1-4-5 in 12 playoff games.

Mottau and Krog were Rangers only briefly. Mottau, a defenseman, played 18 games in 2000–01 with three assists, one game in 2001–02, and spent 1 ½ seasons in Hartford. Mottau later played three seasons with the Devils and two with the Islanders. Krog, a center, played nine games and scored twice in 2006–07. He also played for the Islanders, Thrashers, and Mighty Ducks.

Author's Note: Goalie Robb Stauber (Minnesota) played 39 games for the Hartford affiliate in 1997–98, and went 20-10-6.

7 Patricks.

Five Patricks won the Stanley Cup, with Lester winning three of the four times that the Rangers hoisted the sport's Grail as either coach or general manager: 1928, 1933, and 1940. His sons, Lynn and Frederick Murray (Muzz), were players on the 1940 championship team. Frank Patrick was a coach, player, and general manager for the Vancouver Millionaires, who won the Cup in 1918. And Craig Patrick, Lynn's son, who coached the Rangers for parts of the 1980–81 and 1984–85 seasons, won two as general manager of the Pittsburgh Penguins.

(If the Washington Capitals win the Cup, Muzz's son Dick, the team's president, would make it six Patricks to have that honor.)

Frank and Lester were born to Joseph Patrick, a Canadian lumberman who first suggested putting numbers on players' uniforms and in-game programs to help broadcasters and fans identify skaters.

Those were just one of the dozens of creative moves— from rules to statistics—ushered in by Lester and to some extent, his older brother Frank, that re-engineered and developed the sport, and that remain more than a century later.

The brothers founded the Pacific Coast Hockey Association in 1911 and began to shape the game as we know it today, including opening some of the first indoor arenas in Canada.

Some of the other changes:

- Introducing blue lines and the penalty shot
- Allowing goalies to drop to the ice to make a save
- Crediting assists after a goal
- The boarding penalty
- The playoff system
- Raising a stick after scoring a goal
- Allowing the puck to be kicked anywhere—but not into the net!

With the Rangers, Lester Patrick—for whom an annual award for outstanding service to US hockey is named—is perhaps best known for stepping from the bench to the crease at age 44 after goalie Lorne Chabot suffered an eye injury in Game 2 of the Stanley Cup Finals against Montreal in 1928. The Maroons refused to approve the use of substitute goalies available in the stands, so Patrick pulled on the gear, said "Boys, don't let an old man down," and stopped 18 of 19 shots in a 2-1 overtime win. In that game, he became the oldest player ever to skate in the Finals.

Lynn, a left wing, played 10 seasons with the Rangers and coached 107 games in the 1948–49 and 1949–50 seasons, going 40-51-16, but also helped guide the team to the 1950 Stanley Cup Final. Playing on a line with Bryan Hextall and Phil Watson, Patrick led the NHL with 32 goals

Lester Patrick won three Stanley Cups as either manager, coach, or general manager. This Rangers squad, shown before the 1928–29 season, included (left to right, top row) Billy Boyd, Butch Keeling, Patrick, Ching Johnson, Myles Lane, Taffy Abel, and Paul Thompson. In the first row: trainer Harry Westerby, Murray Murdoch, Frank Councher, Bill Cook, goalie John Ross Roach, Leo Bourgault, and Bun Cook. (AP Photo)

in 1941–42. In 455 games, Patrick scored 145 goals and 335 points.

Muzz, a defenseman, had two stints as coach, a total of 136 games, but was general manager of the Rangers for ten years, from 1955–64.

8 In 1928, Frank Boucher scored at 3:35 of the third period against the Montreal Maroons in Game 5 at the Montreal Forum for a 2-1 win.

Bill Cook scored at 7:34 of overtime in 1933 against the Maple Leafs in Game 4, a 1-0 overtime win at Maple Leaf Gardens.

Bryan Hextall made the list in 1940, against the Leafs in Game 6, a 3-2 overtime win.

From 1928 through 1931, the league's quarterfinals and semifinals—each two games—were decided by goal totals. In 1928, the Rangers split the quarterfinal games, taking control early by winning Game 1 4-0 and edging the Pirates 6-4.

In the semis, they tied Boston at 1 and then won 4-1, advancing to the low-scoring best-of-five Finals. All the games were played in Montreal because the circus was at MSG. The Blueshirts were blanked 2-0 in Games 1 and 3 and won Game 2, 2-1 in overtime. They rebounded to blank the Maroons 1-0 in Game 4. Boucher, who played on the Bread Line with Bill and Bun Cook, was the hero. He led the team in scoring with seven goals and 10 points in the nine games.

In 1933, the Rangers captured the quarterfinals with the Canadiens, winning 5-2 and tying the second game 3-3 to move on to the semifinals in the Detroit Olympia against the Red Wings, who had just changed their name from the Falcons. The Blueshirts swept that series, 2-0 and 4-3.

Again, it was a best-of-five series to bring the Cup home. The Rangers won the first two games, 5-1 and 3-1, but the Leafs fought off elimination in Game 3 with a 3-2 victory. On April 13 in Toronto, Cook scored the deciding goal in overtime. He was the first player to ever decide the final in that fashion. It was Cook's third goal of the playoffs, but Cecil Dillon led all scorers with eight goals in eight games. The winning goalie? Rookie Andy Aitkenhead.

Along came 1940. At Madison Square Garden, the Rangers won the first two games, but because the circus had set up shop there, a common occurrence in that era, the series shifted to Toronto, where they lost twice to the Leafs. Muzz Patrick's overtime goal won Game 5, 2-1, and Hextall's overtime goal, just 2:07 into the extra session of Game 6, sealed the franchise's third Cup, with a 3-2 decision.

Hextall, a left-handed shooter who played right wing—an unusual sight at the time—was no stranger to scoring. He collected 187 goals and 362 points in 449 games. His sons, Bryan Jr. and Dennis, both had long NHL careers, and his grandson, Ron, the former Flyers goaltender, is now the team's general manager.

9 Rick Middleton: Nifty

Why "Nifty?" Well, it rhymes with "Shifty," which fans thought fit Middleton, who would combine subtle moves and fakes in open ice with stick-handling and scoring and was considered one of the best one-on-one players of the late 1970s and early 1980s.

Alf Pike: The Embalmer

In the 1940s, Pike not only played center and defense, he was also a licensed mortician who worked in a funeral home in the offseasons.

Erik Christensen: The Crusher

A thoughtful, sensitive player who was a shootout specialist. In some cases, the nickname reflects the opposite personality.

Ed Hospodar: Boxcar

Why? Because the rugged—and often dirty—defenseman who had a tendency to incite brawls came at players like a runaway train.

Gilles Marotte: Captain Crunch

Built like a fire hydrant, he patrolled the blueline for three years in New York in the mid-1970s and delivered jarring hits.

Don Murdoch: Murder

In his first 14 NHL games, he scored 14 goals and became the toast of the town. Unfortunately, the nightlife short-circuited his promising career.

Clarence Abel: Taffy

Taffy was anything but soft. The hard-hitting defense-man from Michigan loved the chewy confection.

Emile Francis: The Cat

With a small frame, lightning reflexes, and "nine lives"— he could recover quickly after stopping shots—the name was perfect for the future coach and general manager.

Mats Zuccarello: Frodo

Simple: The diminutive winger looked a lot like "The Hobbit" of films, although he was born in Norway, not in Middle Earth.

Cam Talbot: Goalbuster

As Henrik Lundqvist's backup, his mask featured the Zuul Dog, Stay Puft Marshmallow Man, and Sigourney Weaver and Bill Murray from the *Ghostbusters* flick of the 1980s.

Andy Hebenton: Spuds

Don't overthink this one: he liked potatoes.

Frank Beaton: Seldom

A minor-league bomber who threw fists at the drop of a hat, this WHA brawler played just 25 games for the Blueshirts.

10 Mark Pavelich, the center from Minnesota, scored 76 points in the 1981–82 season—the most ever for a Rangers rookie. Though Pavlich is arguably best known for playing on the

Cam Talbot, wearing one of the more unique masks in team lore, deflects away Sean Couturier's shot on Oct. 24, 2013, in Philadelphia. As Henrik Lundqvist's backup before he was traded to Edmonton, Talbot's "Ghostbusters" headgear featured characters from the popular 1980s movie. (AP Photo/Laurence Kesterson)

1980 US Olympic hockey team that won the gold medal in Lake Placid, and assisting on Mike Eruzione's game-winning goal against the Soviet Union.

Pavelich was never drafted. After the "Miracle on Ice," he played one season for HC Lugano in Switzerland, where he collected 73 points in 60 games. That was enough for US Olympic coaches Herb Brooks and Craig Patrick, who had taken charge of the Blueshirts, and knew what the small playmaker could offer, to bring him home.

In his sophomore NHL season, he scored 75 points, with 37 goals and nine points in nine playoff games, usually paired

Former US Olympian Mark Pavelich (16) became the first American to score five goals in a game when the Rangers beat the Hartford Whalers on Feb. 23, 1983, at the Garden, but wasn't always as fortunate that season. This shot from Washington Capitals captain Doug Jarvis (25) banked in off his skate past goalie Glen Hanlon on Dec. 7. (AP Photo/Ron Frehm)

with Ron Duguay, Anders Hedberg, and Rob McClanahan. On February 23, 1983, Pavelich became the first American to score five goals in a game (against the Hartford Whalers at the Garden).

In 1985, when coach Ted Sator ditched Brooks's freewheeling strategy in favor of a dump-and-chase style, Pavelich briefly rejoined Brooks with the Minnesota North Stars before retiring from the NHL.

But it was Tony Granato, another American, who scored the most goals as a rookie. Granato, who was selected by the Rangers in the sixth round (120th overall) in the 1982 Entry Draft, came out of the University of Wisconsin to score 36 goals in the 1988–89 season. It turned out to be his only full season on Broadway: he was traded to Los Angeles in 1990 and finished his career with three more 30-plus-goal seasons before eventually moving to coaching.

11 They have stretched from the northeast to Colorado. They are: Springfield Indians, Philadelphia Ramblers, New York Rovers, Providence Reds, Baltimore Clippers, St. Paul Rangers, Omaha Knights, Buffalo Bisons, New Haven Nighthawks, Denver/Colorado Rangers, Binghamton Rangers. Here's a little info about each one:

Springfield (Mass.) Indians (1926–33 and 1959–62)

The Canadian-American Hockey League was founded in Springfield in 1926; the Indians were one of the five franchises. It was run at the time by Lester Patrick. Charlie Rayner, Earl Siebert, Cecil Dillon, and Ott Heller were among those who would later be called up to the Rangers. The pinnacle of the franchise came from 1959–62, however, when the Indians won three straight Calder Cups, losing only five playoff games. Goaltender Marcel Paille and Bill Sweeney, who won the league scoring title all three years, led the squad.

Philadelphia Ramblers (1935–41)

Several players from the 1940 Stanley Cup championship team came from here, including Bryan Hextall Sr., Kilby Mac-Donald, Neil Lowell, and Phil Watson. The squad played in the Philadelphia Arena.

New York Rovers (1935–1948)

More than 75 players from the Eastern Amateur Hockey League Rovers and its later incarnations skated in the NHL, including Gilles Villemure, Ed Giacomin, Alf Pike, Muzz Patrick, and Fred Shero. After folding the franchise, the team was resurrected in 1959, playing in the Long Island Arena, and changed its name to the Long Island Ducks in 1961. The revived Rovers—of the Eastern League—played at Madison Square Garden in 1964–65, concluded with a 25-39-8 record, and did not make the playoffs.

Baltimore Clippers (1962–67)

Among the alumni from this AHL club: Val Fonteyne, Bill Hicke, Cesare Maniago, and Ken Schinkel.

St. Paul (Minnesota) Rangers (1963–66)

They were in the Central Professional Hockey League, and when the Minnesota North Stars were awarded an expansion team, the Rangers switched to Omaha in 1967.

Omaha Knights (1966–72)

They were the Central Hockey League champs in 1969–70 and 1970–71. Larry Popein, a Rangers center from 1954 to 1961, was coach for the first championship and Fred Shero for the second.

Buffalo Bisons (1967–70)

The team ceased operations after the 1969–70 season because the NHL expanded to include the Sabres, who began playing in 1970–71. Goaltender Roger Crozier played eight games for the Bisons and eight years for the Sabres.

Providence Reds (1971–76)

This AHL team's name came from the breed of chicken known as the Rhode Island Red and eventually morphed into the Binghamton Dusters, Whalers, and Rangers.

New Haven Nighthawks (1976–81, 1984–87)

Among the future NHLers: Bernie Nicholls, Mike Rogers, Doug Soetaert.

Colorado/Denver Rangers (1987–89)

In their first season, they were called the Colorado Rangers of the International Hockey League, switched to Denver in the second, then folded. In those two years, an array of future New York Rangers passed through, some for a cup of coffee in the NHL and others who played far longer. They include: Ulf Dahlen, Marcel Dionne, Ron Duguay, Tony Granato, Kevin Miller, Darren Turcotte, John Ogrodnick, Rudy Poeschek, Simon Wheeldon, and Brad Stepan, the father of Derek Stepan.

Binghamton Rangers (1990–97)

A popular attraction in upstate New York at the Broome County Veterans Memorial Arena, these are some of the alumni: Daniel Lacroix, Tie Domi, Dan Cloutier, Par Djoos, Chris and Peter Ferraro, Mattias Norstrom, and Sergei Zubov.

12 Mention "Stemmer" to Rangers fans of a certain age, and you'll get a smile and a story.

More often than not, the topic will be Pete Stemkowski's triple-overtime goal in Game 6 of the Stanley Cup Final in 1971 at Madison Square Garden, an electrifying moment that put the Rangers on the brink of sipping from the Silver Chalice.

A Winnipeg native, Stemkowski was 27 at the time, a third-line center behind Jean Ratelle and Walt Tkaczuk with a penchant for winning faceoffs and friends.

Known as "The Polish Prince," Stemkowski—who won a Cup in 1967 with the Toronto Maple Leafs—was traded to the Rangers by Detroit general manager Ned Harkness on

Halloween, October 31, 1970, for defenseman Larry Brown. He's said many times that Manhattan was a culture shock for him, and moved to Long Beach on Long Island, where many teammates lived and car-pooled into the city for games.

The new landscape didn't change Stemmer. Once when the team bus was driving through a seedy section of East St. Louis, they passed the rubble of a burned-out school. To break the tension, Stemmer piped up: "Looks like someone failed chemistry."

On the ice, Stemkowski's performances were no laughing matter. In seven seasons on Broadway, he scored 20 or more goals from 1972–73 to 1974–75, and tied his career high of 25 in 1973–74. In that season, he also produced a career-high 70 points.

In the spring of 1971, however, Stemkowski had scored the ones that counted.

In Game 1 in Chicago, on April 18, 1971, Stemkowski scored at 1:37 of the first overtime to give the Blueshirts a 2-1 victory and 1-0 lead in the best-of-seven series. But the Hawks would eventually lead the series 3-2 when they came to New York for Game 6 11 days later. The Rangers hadn't been to the Finals in 21 years, so the Garden Faithful were hungry.

Stemkowski stepped up. The Hawks and Rangers were tied at 2, and had skated more than 40 extra minutes. "I was playing on fumes," Stemmer remembered. "But I can still see a Stan Mikita shot that hit both posts and [Rangers defenseman] Rod Seiling golfing it away."

For fans who don't know how the game-winner unfolded, Stemkowski will "kid around . . . . I tell them it was an end-to-end rush and that I deked the goalie and put it top corner."

Not really. Defenseman Tim Horton fired a long shot that goalie Tony Esposito stopped. Both Ted Irvine and then

Stemkowski went to the crease, but it was No. 21 who poked it into the net. It was the first ever scored by a Ranger after two overtimes. But the fairy tale ending never materialized. In Game 7, Stemkowski scored another goal to tie the score at 1, but the Black Hawks eliminated the Rangers 4-2.

The Blueshirts would make a run to the Finals the following season, but fell to Boston in six games. In all, Stemmer was 113-204-317 in 496 regular-season games for the Rangers and scored 18 goals in 55 postseason tilts.

It would be decades before another triple-overtime winner would occur. In Washington on May 2, 2012, Marian Gaborik's shot propelled the Rangers over the Capitals in Game 3 of their series in the Eastern Conference Semifinals. Stemkowski was watching. Maybe there was some magic in the air.

13 In 1995, members of the Stanley Cup team—Glen Healy, Mike Richter, Joey Kocur, Nick Kypreos, Eddie Olczyk, Jeff Beukeboom, Adam Graves, Brian Leetch, and Mark Messier— were filmed at practice and asked how they spent their summer vacation. There's some worthwhile behind-the-scenes chatter.

Before the 2009 season, at CBS studios, ten Rangers read—rather woodenly—"Things That You Wouldn't Hear a Hockey Player Say." They were Sean Avery, Henrik Lundqvist, Ryan Callahan, Chris Drury, Christopher Higgins, Marc Staal, Brandon Dubinsky, Marian Gaborik, Dan Girardi, and Donald Brashear.

The funniest Letterman segment was in 1984 when Dave Maloney helped Letterman suit up as a goalie, instructing him on how to guard the net, telling stories, and then scoring almost at will.

On second thought, look them all up on You Tube.

14 Emile Francis has by far the most regular-season victories, with 342. Lester Patrick is second with 281. Alain Vigneault is third, and closing in on 200. Frank Boucher has 181.

If all goes according to plan, those four will eventually have more than 1,000 combined.

Now for perspective: The top 10 coaches had 1,835 total wins through the 2016–17 regular season. The bottom 24 coaches on the list, including Fred Shero, Mike Keenan, and Glen Sather, had 903 total. Many of those coaches were short-timers, with 14 winning less than 40 games.

Emile Francis cheers after the Rangers scored in the second period in an April 24, 1974, playoff game against the Flyers in Philadelphia. Francis holds the record for the most regular-season victories (342) behind the Blueshirts bench. (AP Photo/Brian Horton)

Top 10

- Emile Francis 342
- Lester Patrick 281
- Alain Vigneault 192 (still active)
- Frank Boucher 181
- John Tortorella 171
- Tom Renney 164
- Roger Neilson 141
- Herb Brooks 131
- Phil Watson 119
- Colin Campbell 118

So there is undeniably clear separation in the pages of the history of bench bosses.

When you consider playoff wins, which some believe is more important, as well as winning percentage, the top three are the same, but Mike Keenan, who coached one magnificent season, Fred Shero, and Lynn Patrick rise on the list.

Playoff Wins

- Emile Francis 34
- Lester Patrick 32
- Alain Vigneault 31
- John Tortorella 19
- Colin Campbell 18
- Mike Keenan 16
- Fred Shero 15

Winning Percentage

- Mike Keenan .696
- Lynn Patrick .583
- Fred Shero .556

- Alain Vigneault .508
- Colin Campbell .500
- Herb Brooks .500
- Ted Sator .500

Yes, Francis, Tortorella, and Renney are among those below .500.

15 Alexander Karpovtsev, Alexei Kovalev, Sergei Nemchinov, and Sergei Zubov.

A rookie defenseman on the Stanley Cup–winning team in 1994, Karpotsev had three goals and 15 assists with a plus-minus of 12 that season. After being drafted by the Quebec Nordiques in 1990, Karpotsev was obtained by General Manager Neil Smith, who was enamored with some Russians players, in 1993. Sergei Nemchinov, Alexei Kovalev, and Sergei Zubov were also amongst the influx. Karpotsev played 12 seasons in the NHL with the Rangers, Toronto, Chicago, the Islanders, and Florida until injuries limited and finally curtailed his career.

Karpotsev, 41, died in the September 7, 2011, plane crash in Russia that claimed most of Lokomotiv Yaroslavl, the Kontinental Hockey League team. He was an assistant coach.

Kovalev, who was 20 years old in the 1993–94 campaign, started his 20-plus-season career with a bang, scoring 23 goals and 56 points in 76 games during the regular season and had a superb postseason, with nine goals and 12 assists in 23 games on the path to the Cup.

Kovalev didn't always see eye-to-eye with coach Mike Keenan, known as "Iron Mike." On February 23, 1994, a day before his birthday, he extended his shift for more than a minute, and Keenan was irritated and decided to teach him a lesson. Keenan wouldn't let him back on the bench, and Kovalev finished the period on a seven-plus-minute shift. It backfired: Kovalev drew two penalties and scored a goal.

A terrific offensive player with strength and skill, Kovalev—who was drafted 15th overall in 1991, scored 430 goals and 1,029 points, primarily with the Rangers, Penguins, and Canadiens; he finished his career with the Senators and Panthers.

Nemchinov, a Moscow native, was a valuable two-way center who had dressed for the Central Red Army team as a junior and served on the national team. The Rangers picked him 244th overall in the 1990 draft and he began his career

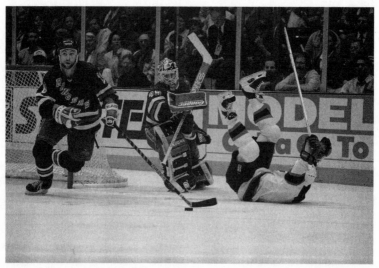

Defenseman Sergei Zubov, drafted by the Blueshirts in 1990 and one of the first Russians to have his name inscribed on the Cup, left, skates away with the puck near Rangers goaltender Mike Richter during overtime on May 19, 1994, against the Devils in Meadowlands Arena. (AP Photo/Bill Kostroun)

when he was freed of his contracts in Russia. He scored 22 goals and 49 points in the Cup championship season in 1994, and later in his career, won a second Cup with the Devils in 2000.

Like Nemchinov, Zubov was drafted by the Blueshirts in 1990, but he evolved into a significant blueliner, talented offensively and above average defensively. He is the NHL's second all-time leading scorer among Russian defensemen, and also won a Cup with the Dallas Stars in 1999.

16 This club is so exclusive that only six players belong, and it's doubtful that there will be a seventh anytime soon.

Jaromir Jagr, 123 points (54-69) in 2005–06, an amazing season for the ageless Czech star.

Jean Ratelle, 109 points (46-63) in 1971–72—and he broke his ankle and missed 17 games.

Mark Messier, 107 points (35-72) in 1991–92, when he won the Hart Trophy.

Vic Hadfield, 106 points (50-56; the first Ranger to reach 50 goals) in 1971–72, after he tried a curved stick blade a la Bobby Hull.

Mike Rogers, 103 points (38-65), in 1981–82, a terrific skater who had played in Hartford with Gordie and Mark Howe.

Brian Leetch, 102 points (22-80) in 1991–92, when he had a streak of 23 assists in 15 games.

17 It was November 2, 1975, one of the most emotional nights in Garden history.

Veteran Eddie Giacomin, who had anchored the Rangers' crease since 1965, was wearing No. 31 in Red Wings red, not his No. 1 in blue, and the entire evening was a rousing tribute to a blue-collar leader, a captain without the "C," who had been waived and claimed by Detroit for $30,000.

Giacomin, who was 36 and had been considering retiring when he was waived, instead decided to make his Wings debut several days later against the team that "threw me to the wolves like a piece of garbage."

Greeted by a prolonged standing ovation and chants of "Ed-die, Ed-die, Ed-die," a response that made the veteran net-minder wipe his eyes before donning his mask, he put forth a vintage performance.

The Wings burst out to a 4-0 lead and Giacomin stopped four breakaways in a 6-4 victory. "He didn't beat us with his goaltending, he beat us with his presence," said defenseman Brad Park.

"Players had a lot of difficulty playing against him," said Steve Vickers, who was booed by 17,500 fans for scoring on their hero.

It wasn't an isolated incident, but still outraged the fan base. General manager Emile Francis had been cleaning house. The deal was the third in four days and the swaps included goalie Gilles Villemure and center Derek Sanderson. The Rangers brought Dunc Wilson up to back up Davidson, the 22-year-old goalie. (Now there's an obscure piece of trivia.)

Davidson, who was just starting his career—which would later continue as a Rangers and NBC analyst and an NHL executive—was rendered speechless by the news.

After all, a greying Giacomin was in his 11th season with the Blueshirts, the only NHL team for which he had donned the mask, gloves, and pads. He had been a fixture, waving to fans and talking to them on the streets of the city, besides appearing in 538 games, plus 65 playoff matches. That was more than any other goalie in franchise history, and could be considered the soul of the club.

Davidson later told of flying to Montreal for a game, and wondering why Giacomin wasn't in his usual spot in the back of the plane. He found a stunned trainer Frank Paice and asked.

"He's not here," Davidson recalled Paice saying. "He was waived and claimed by Detroit." Davidson was speechless. "I had no clue anything was coming. I was brought in to (as a backup) support Eddie and then suddenly there I was, the No. 1 goaltender in New York City. And two days later, here comes Eddie with the Red Wings. It was surreal."

18 Decades before the tong wars between those current squads, a pitched 15-year battle was waged in Manhattan. Imagine the rivalry between a younger and older brother in the same house, vying for attention, elbows askew, fighting for territory.

From 1927 to 1942, that was the intensity of the clashes between the New York Americans and the Rangers, who shared the ice at the original Madison Square Garden.

"It was like a civil war, said Muzz Patrick, who played in 16 games against the Amerks as a Ranger. "Landlords against the tenants. The aristocrats against the people's choice."

One of the city's more infamous bootleggers, William "Big Bill" Dwyer bought the Hamilton minor-league franchise for $75,000 and the Amerks, with their star-spangled jerseys, rented the Garden first, in 1925. But when boxing promoter "Tex" Rickard founded the Rangers in May 1926, he moved them into the building on 50th and Eighth as well.

The Rangers won the Cup in 1928 and earned a playoff berth for nine straight seasons; the Amerks were the sibling, the t-shirt to the bow tie. The rivalry divided the fan base because familiar names flocked to the Amerks: Montreal forward Nels Stewart, known as Old Poison; Maple Leafs captain Clarence (Hap) Day and former Rangers defenseman Ching Johnson.

In the 1937–38 season, the teams met in the first playoff round, a best-of-three series with no road games.

With the series tied at a game apiece, the one that would send the winner to the Stanley Cup Final started at 8:30 pm on March 27, 1938, and ended at 1:30 the next morning.

In the fourth overtime, Lorne Carr, a swift little right wing, who earned the name Sudden Death after this marathon, beat goalie Dave Kerr for the 3-2 win. It was the first time that a hockey game made the front page of the *New York Times*.

19 The Rangers had taken Game 1 in Montreal, where the Canadiens had won three straight Cups, and Montreal coach Scotty Bowman was going to replace Ken Dryden in Game 2 with backup Michel "Bunny" Larocque, who had relieved Dryden for the third period of the first game and blanked the Blueshirts.

But Larocque, who hadn't started any of the previous 64 playoff games, was knocked unconscious during the warmups by an errant shot from Doug Risebrough that hit him in the mask and left him lying on the ice at the Montreal Forum. He was taken to the hospital and Dryden drew back into the lineup.

It started well for the Rangers in Game 2. Anders Hedberg and Ron Duguay scored in the first 6:21, but Dryden stiffened and the Canadiens took over. Dryden allowed only five more goals in the series and the Canadiens rose to the occasion: 6-2, 4-1, 4-3, and 4-1.

"We just died. We stopped. We went in reverse," said Phil Esposito. "We took a 2-0 lead in the second game and never won another faceoff."

John Davidson, who had injured his knee against the Islanders—requiring major offseason surgery—had helped the Blueshirts get to Montreal with an outstanding series. Davidson stopped 64 of 66 shots in the two wins against the Kings, and only eight goals in five games against the Flyers. Ron Greschner scored a power-play goal in overtime to win Game 6 in the semifinals against the Islanders to advance the Rangers to the Final.

Former Bruin Esposito said he told coach Fred Shero to move the team to a suburban hotel to avoid the nightlife and temptations of one of Canada's most seductive and appealing cities. Shero refused, Esposito said.

20 Thanks to goaltender Chuck Rayner, who teammates called "The Lone Ranger," this group, coached by Lynn Patrick, finished fourth in the six-team league. It was in the first round, against the Canadiens, that our first name emerged as a hero.

Rayner, who was adept at puck-handling and sometimes tried to score goals, a brash feat. But why not? The Rangers weren't an offensive powerhouse, and Rayner won the Hart Trophy that season as the league's most valuable player, which is remarkable, considering his record was 28-30-11. In fact, when he was inducted into the Hall of Fame in 1973, he was only the second goaltender with a losing record in his career to be honored.

Lund, the forward who scored the first goal by a Finn in the NHL and became the first star from that country, scored five goals in the five-game series that the Blueshirts won. Not only were the goals noteworthy, but Lund, who had been awarded the Calder Trophy as top rookie in 1948–1949, shadowed the iconic Maurice "Rocket" Richard, holding him to one goal in the series.

For another spring, the Rangers were evicted from the Garden for the Final against the Red Wings because the building was booked for the wildly popular and immensely lucrative Ringling Bros. circus, and chose to play their two designated "home" games at Maple Leafs Gardens.

The Garden corporation could make more money when the lions and elephants and clowns and acrobats came to town in the spring. This forced the Rangers, and later the New York Knicks, to use different arenas.

Remember, at the time, arenas were configured differently: a circus and a game couldn't take place on the same day.

Playing without Gordie Howe, their injured superstar, the Red Wings won the opening game, 4-1, in the Detroit Olympia, and the teams split the next pair at Maple Leaf Gardens.

Enter our third name: Don Raleigh.

Raleigh, a center known as "Bones," scored the sudden-death overtime winners in Games 4 and 5 at the Olympia.

In Game 4, with the Rangers down in games 2-1, Raleigh managed to sweep the puck past goalie Harry Lumley while falling to the ice about nine minutes in. In Game 5, Raleigh didn't wait that long: his short shot won it about 90 seconds into the extra session.

The sudden-death exploits didn't prompt the nickname. Historian Stan Fischler tells this story: after winning some dough at Belmont racetrack on Long Island on a horse named "Bag of Bones" and having a big game that night, *Journal-American* writer Barney Kremenko simply shortened it for Raleigh.

After the Blueshirts took a 3-2 series lead, the NHL stepped in and ruled that the deciding game in a Stanley Cup Final could not be played on neutral ice. The Maple Leaf Gardens was "neutral" because its tenants were the Leafs.

The circus was still at Madison Square Garden, so the Detroit Olympia was thus the locale for the sixth (although the Rangers were to be designated the "home" team for that match) and seventh games, both of which were won by the Wings.

Babando was not a Ranger—well, not at that time. The Braeburn, Pennsylvania, native was a forward for the Wings, and he denied the Blueshirts the Cup.

Off a faceoff, his backhand shot from the left circle at 8:30 of the second overtime of Game 7 deflected off a player, changed direction, and flew low past Rayner into the far corner of the net. And just like that, he stepped into the annals of hockey history.

Three years later, Babando, who had been traded to the Chicago Blackhawks, was sold to—yep, the Rangers—with whom he played 29 games and scored four of the 86 goals in his career.

Naturally, none was more memorable than the one in Game 7, more than half a century ago.

"Not a day goes by that I don't think about that goal," Rayner once recalled. "What a shame that was. Just one goal and there never would have been a 54-year drought."

SECOND PERIOD

In hockey, the second period is like a transition. During intermission, coaches make adjustments and players discuss what needs to change. Teams can build on a strong first period or recover from a lousy one. But it's not easy. Each team has watched videos of the opponent's strategy to gain an edge; maybe some players have been banged up. So the second period can be a tipping point. Good luck with these questions, some of which may have multiple parts . . .

1 Which Boston Bruins led a post-game charge into the stands during the famous brawl at Madison Square Garden on December 23, 1979? And which frenzied player struck one fan with his own shoe? *Answer on page 81.*

2 Which Ranger shot the puck that forced Jacques Plante to become the first goaltender to wear a mask regularly for the first time? Hint: He once held the Rangers record for career goals before he was traded. *Answer on page 83.*

3 Olli Jokinen came from the Calgary Flames and played just 26 regular-season games. What will Rangers fans always remember him for? *Answer on page 85.*

4 The California Golden Seals, a team that entered the NHL as simply the California Seals in 1967 and then became the Oakland Seals, were rarely golden against the Rangers. In fact, two of the biggest routs in franchise

history took place when the Seals visited the Garden. Can you guess the scores? *Answer on page 87.*

5 Let's take it to the other extreme. What were the worst losses suffered by your beloved Blueshirts? *Answer on page 88.*

6 The NHL truly has evolved into an international sport, growing across borders and generating interest. The 2016–17 Rangers were a good example of the array of homelands. At least nine countries were represented on the roster at some point during the season. Name the countries and the players. *Answer on page 89.*

7 Fans of a certain age—or those who have seen photographs—recall the distinctive marquee at the third Garden that was crammed with abbreviations about upcoming events.

For example: AFT-KNICKS v/s LAKERS EVE-ECAC BASKETBALL RHODE IS U v/s ST. JOE N WESTERN v/s PROV TOM'W-RANGERS v/s DET

Two well-known establishments bookended the Garden entrance. What were they? *Answer on page 89.*

8 A goalie and a classical pianist, he believed in reincarnation and his roaring tiger mask set a standard. Who was this masked man? *Answer on page 90.*

9 Long before Glen Sather became the architect of the Edmonton Oilers dynasty—and later took his ever-present stogie to Manhattan—the left wing spent some time in a Rangers uniform. How did Slats get here? *Answer on page 91.*

10 You might think that Brian Leetch, the keeper of almost all offensive records for defensemen, scored the most

goals by a blueliner in a given season. You would be wrong. In 1984–85, this fellow had 28. Coach Herb Brooks called him the best skater in the NHL. Who is he? *Answer on page 93.*

11 In what year did the Rangers add a white jersey to their classic blue (hence the nickname "Broadway Blueshirts")? Hint: Harry S. Truman was president and electric guitar pioneer Les Paul (and Mary Ford) had the hit single "How High the Moon." *Answer on page 94.*

12 In three separate deals just prior to the NHL trade deadline in 1994, the Blueshirts acquired four players who would turn out to the critical in the quest for the Cup. Who were they and from where did they come? *Answer on page 95.*

13 The Rangers' first road game was in Toronto. But they didn't play the Maple Leafs. Who were the opponents? *Answer on page 96.*

14 Who dubbed Mark Messier "Mr. June," a reference to Yankee Reggie Jackson's nickname "Mr. October?" *Answer on page 97.*

15 Who led the Rangers in penalty minutes for a single season?

    Part II: Name the Rangers' top five players in career penalty minutes. Hint: The top four are defensemen. Who was the forward? *Answer on page 97.*

16 I starred and won two Cups wearing No. 7, which was later retired in honor of Rod Gilbert. An NHL trophy was created for gentlemanly play and I won it more times than anyone. And in the mid-1940s, I was the first

coach to alternate goalies every game. Who am I? *Answer on page 101.*

17 There are two versions of The Curse—the hex that supposedly doomed the Rangers to wait 54 years to win the Stanley Cup after the 1940 championship. What's the tale of one, or both? *Answer on page 104.*

18 Which unlikely player, making his NHL debut, helped break the Montreal Canadiens' 28-game winning streak in 1978? *Answer on page 107.*

19 What's a professional sport without television, right? In what year and from where was the first hockey game broadcast in the United States? Bonus: One of those teams later played in the first national NHL broadcast in the US. When was that? *Answer on page 108.*

20 The Foreigner hit song "Double Vision," which also was the title of the album that went platinum in a week, was written based on a Rangers event. Which one? *Answer on page 109.*

21 Speaking of seeing double, there were quite a lot of second takes when the Rangers faced the Stars in Dallas on December 14, 2006. Why? *Answer on page 112.*

22 Only two Rangers have ever scored five goals in a game. They are _____ and _____. *Answer on page 117.*

SECOND PERIOD— ANSWERS

1 Terry O'Reilly and Peter McNab led a swarm of B's into the lower bowl. Mike Milbury joined in and smacked a fan with his footwear.

The confrontation, which resulted in suspension, fines, and lawsuits, was one of the highest-profile altercations between fans and athletes in any sport at the time, and began soon after the Bruins beat the Blueshirts 4-3.

When time ran out in the belligerent match, which was normal in the days of the so-called "Big Bad Bruins" and in the era when on-ice fights seemed to occur every game, Rangers center Phil Esposito smashed his stick on the ice after not cashing in what would have been a tying breakaway in the final seconds and Bruins left wing Al Secord sucker-punched Ulf Nilsson after the horn.

Rangers goaltender John Davidson left his crease and skated to the end of the rink to confront Secord, and the already angry crowd roared.

A scrum developed and Secord and Ranger Frank Beaton appeared ready to square off. Then, a 30-year-old fan, John Kaptain, reached over the glass—the transparent protective shield was lower then—smacked Stan Jonathan in the face with a rolled-up program, and pulled away the Bruin enforcer's stick. He told reporters that one of the players had hit his brother, James.

O'Reilly, a grinder who never backed down and was involved in 22 fights during games that season, scaled the plexiglass to get at Kaptain, who was waving Jonathan's stick. McNab, a far more peaceful player, nonetheless joined O'Reilly, and most of the Bruins followed.

Milbury, a 27-year-old defenseman, and goaltender Gerry Cheevers, were already in the locker room and heard the commotion. Milbury went back into the rink and up the stairs into the crowd. "I went from happy and content, and ready to go home for Christmas, to full combat mode in about 20 seconds," Milbury said. Cheevers declined involvement, saying later: "I was already on my second beer."

By that point, O'Reilly had bear-hugged Kaptain, fans surrounded them, and security guards began to move in. With O'Reilly trying to fend off the fans, Kaptain tried to flee up the steps, but was pinned across a seat by McNab.

Enter Milbury, a former general manager and coach of the Islanders and now a studio analyst for NBC.

"I grabbed his shoe, took a little tug on it," Milbury recalled on the 30th anniversary of the melee. "I gave him a cuff across the leg, and then I did what I thought was probably the most egregious thing of all: I threw his shoe on the ice."

O'Reilly, who later coached the Bruins and was an assistant coach in New York, was suspended eight games. McNab—also a long-time broadcaster—and Milbury were banned for six each. They were each fined $500 and the rest of the Bruins, except for Cheevers, were fined up to $500.

The NHL also ordered that higher glass be installed around the league to prevent other incidents.

The Kaptains, their father, Manny, and a friend, Jack Guttenplan, were charged with disorderly conduct, but the charges were eventually dismissed. The family withdrew a lawsuit, and the Manhattan district attorney chose not to press charges against the players.

2 Andy Bathgate.

A prolific scorer who possessed one of the hardest slap shots in a league dominated by wristers—he holds the team record for a 10-game goal streak and in 1958–59, was the first Blueshirt to score 40 goals in a season—Bathgate also had a mean streak.

Andy Bathgate, celebrating his 33rd goal on March 1, 1959, would score seven more to become the first Ranger to notch 40 in a season. Bathgate, who also holds the team record for scoring in consecutive games—10—died in 2016. (AP Photo/Marty Lederhandler)

Early in the 1959–60 season, when no goaltenders wore face gear, a maskless Plante, guarding the nets for the Montreal Canadiens, tripped him with a poke-check. "I went headfirst into the boards and I cut my ear and cut my face a little," Bathgate told Turner Sports Network in 2009.

Believing he could have been severely hurt, the Winnipeg native didn't forget. On November 1, 1959, at Madison Square Garden, Bathgate skated down left wing early in the first period. "I was trying to hit him somewhere where he'd remember me and boom, I nailed him."

Bathgate leaned into his dangerous backhand, came in close, and fired through a screen. The puck opened a jagged cut from Plante's nostril to his lips. He crumpled, with blood collecting in a pool. After being escorted to the locker room, and as he was stitched up, Plante came to a ground-breaking decision.

He told Habs coach Toe Blake that he would be wearing a grotesque, cream-colored, plexiglass mask with holes for each eye and his mouth that he had tested during practices. Blake balked, contending that Plante would not see pucks at his skates. Plante refused to budge.

After 21 minutes, play resumed and the Canadiens won 3-1. Plante played the rest of the season wearing the mask, becoming the first NHL goalie to wear one regularly.

Montreal Maroons goalie Clint Benedict, known as "Praying Benny" because he dropped to his knees to block shots, which was illegal at the time, was the first NHL goalie to wear facial protection—modified leather masks—for five games during the 1929–30 season.

After a shot by Howie Morenz broke his nose, sidelining him for six weeks, Benedict began to experiment. His last game wearing a mask was on March 4, when his nose was bloodied during a scrum at the crease and he had to leave the ice. "The nosepiece proved to be the problem, because it obscured my vision," he said.

Thirty years later, Plante kept his mask—and his stand-up style and precision positioning—and won or shared the Vezina Trophy four more times, bringing his total to seven.

Bathgate, who was named Rangers captain in 1961, also rolled on. He played in every regular-season game from 1958–64. During the 1961–62 season, Bathgate led the league in assists and tied Bobby Hull as the league leader in total points, with 28 goals and 56 assists. But Hull won the Art Ross Trophy, because he had more goals (50).

When Bathgate was traded to the Maple Leafs in a block-buster deal, he held every major team scoring record. He was on the Stanley Cup championship team for the Leafs that season. He later played for the Red Wings and the Pittsburgh Penguins, who selected him in the 1967 expansion draft. He had 349 goals and 624 assists in 17 seasons.

Perhaps the most amazing thing about Bathgate was that he played with a steel plate in his left knee that he damaged as a junior player in Guelph, Ontario.

Bathgate held the Rangers record for goals with 272, before Rod Gilbert passed him in 1973. He won the Hart Trophy as the NHL's most valuable player in 1959 after scoring a career-high 40 goals. His No. 9 was raised to the rafters on February 26, 2009, and he died in 2016 at age 83.

3 In one play, Olli Jokinen crushed the playoff hopes of the Blueshirts on the final day of the 2010 regular season in Philadelphia.

The Blueshirts desperately needed a shootout goal from the big Finnish center to prevent the Rangers, who were on a 7-1-2 run, from missing the postseason for the first time in five years. They had caught the slumping Flyers, making up 10 points in three weeks, so it was win-or-go-home.

Henrik Lundqvist, with 46 saves through regulation and overtime, had allowed the Rangers to send the critical game to sudden-death after a 1-1 tie.

P.A. Parenteau's shot had eluded Flyers goaltender Brian Boucher during the shootout, but Boucher stopped Erik Christensen. Danny Briere and Claude Giroux had beaten Lundqvist, so it was up to Jokinen, who had arrived from Calgary with Brandon Prust for Ales Kotalik and Christopher Higgins at the trade deadline, and scored four goals and added 11 assists down the stretch.

But Jokinen, 31, couldn't cash in when it counted.

With the crowd at Wachovia Center standing, Jokinen, who was very successful in shootouts with a 38.9 success rate, slowly circled deep on the left side of the Rangers defensive zone to pick up speed, grabbed the waiting puck at the red line, and sped in. He deked and tried to slide a backhander between Boucher's pads.

Boucher held his ground and stopped it easily.

The fans roared, the Flyers' bench exploded, and the dejected Rangers walked silently into the dressing room. "I'm just so empty, I don't know what to say," Lundqvist said afterward.

It would be the last shot that Jokinen would attempt as a Ranger.

His departure from Calgary would last just five months; he agreed to a two-year contract with the Flames that July.

Jokinen would play for 10 teams before retiring in 2015 and score 321 goals in 1,231 games. He retired as a Florida Panther in March 2017.

Five years earlier, one more goal may have made a world of difference.

4 On November 21, 1971, the Rangers rocked the Seals 12-1, setting a single-game franchise record and a team record for goals in a period: 8.

Gilles Meloche was the goaltender for the Seals that night, when the Rangers scored the first four goals of the game (Jean Ratelle, Vic Hadfield, Ted Irvine, and Ratelle again) before Norm Ferguson scored a disputed goal late in the second period. That call angered the Blueshirts, who turned it up a notch and scored the next eight in the third. Ratelle, Gene Carr, and Pierre Jarry all scored twice, Irvine scored another, and Bill Fairbairn ended the Seals' misery at 19:49. Only one goal was on the power play. Meloche was pulled after goal No. 9. In the locker room afterward, Seals captain Joey Johnston was quoted as saying, "Who's the [bleep] that scored and pissed them off?"

Three years later, on November 17, 1974, the Blueshirts sank the Seals 10-0. That game had the most goals scored while posting a shutout in franchise history, and it was the second time in franchise history the Blueshirts defeated an opponent by 10 or more goals.

Rick Middleton tied a single-game franchise rookie record with four goals and five points. Jerry Butler had two goals. Pete Stemkowski had a goal and three assists, and Ratelle, Rod Gilbert, and Brad Park scored. Goalie Gary Simmons took the bullet for the Seals that night. Gilles Villemure had the two easy nights in net for the Rangers.

5 Poor Tubby McAuley. It's worth repeating when you're having a bad day. Poor Tubby McAuley.

The Rangers netminder, whose first name was Ken, was the victim of a 15-0 onslaught at the Detroit Olympia on January 23, 1944, the worst shellacking in league history.

McAuley, who was one of the wartime replacements for "Sugar" Jim Henry, who was in the Canadian armed forces, was pointed toward the net along with keepers such as Bill Beveridge, Lionel Bouvrette, and Steve Buzinski, whose nickname, author and historian Stan Fischler cackles, was "The Puck Goes Inski."

Tubby's experience came from senior hockey teams such as the Edmonton Maple Leafs and Regina Rangers, but he faced the Wings that fateful night supported by an equally questionable smorgasbord of teammates, with a roster thinned by military service.

The white flag could have been hoisted at the end of two periods: It was 8-0 Wings, and seven more goals were added, although Fischler notes that some believe a 16th crossed the goal line before—not after—the final horn. McAuley had faced 62 shots—he had no replacement in sight—and ended up playing all 50 games that season. He won six and finished with an abominable goals-against-average of 6.20.

There was another forgettable Rangers rout on March 16, 1957, at Maple Leafs Gardens in Toronto. The Leafs beat Gump Worsley, who faced 47 shots, 14-1 to set the record for most Toronto goals in a game.

It was 10-zip in the third period before Ron Murphy scored on a power play.

Hockey's a strange game. Just a week earlier in Toronto, the Rangers had won 2-1.

6 There were numerous Americans (including Ryan McDonagh, Derek Stepan, Chris Kreider, Jimmy Vesey, and Kevin Hayes), Canadians (including Rick Nash, Dan Girardi, and Marc Staal), and Swedes (starting with Henrik Lundqvist, Mika Zibanejad, Jesper Fast, and Oscar Lindberg).

That's the easy three nations. In fact, players from those three countries comprised about 82 percent of the league in 2016–17: Canada 47.1 percent, US 26 percent, Sweden 9 percent. By the last years of the 1980s, the share of Canadians had been about 75 percent.

Three others are slightly tougher. Pavel Buchnevich is Russian, Antti Raanta is from Finland, and Mats Zuccarello is Norwegian.

Now, the final three, all forwards:

Michael Grabner was born in Austria, Marek Hrivik is from Slovakia, and Nicklas Jensen is one of the few players from Denmark to play in the NHL.

Call it diversity:

Grabner was born in Villach, moved to the US to play for Spokane when he was 17, and was drafted by the Vancouver Canucks. As a rookie with the Islanders in 2010–11, he led all first-year players with 34 goals. Hrivik, born in Zilina, has spent most of his time in the organization with the Hartford Wolf Pack. Jensen was born in Herning, but has dual citizenship: his father, Dan, who was born in Toronto, played for the Danish national team. Currently, there are about a dozen Danes in the NHL.

7 Adam Hats was on the left and Nedick's on the right.

Pork-pie hats, fedoras, or straw hats for the summer? Adam, which was a sponsor of the Garden's boxing matches, had them all in their display windows. The company, which also had a store on Fifth Avenue, used fighters and celebrities in their promotions, often on matchbooks.

Nedick's, which sponsored Knicks broadcasts, was a popular fast-food chain that began selling an orange drink—hence the orange-and-white décor—before expanding its menu to include doughnuts, coffee, and signature hot dogs with mustard relish on a toasted bun. "Good like Nedick's" was radio announcer Marty Glickman's catchphrase after a basket.

8 Meet Gilles Gratton, AKA "The Count" or Gratoonie the Loony.

A Quebec native, he played 41 games for the Blueshirts in the 1976–77 season and wore a fierce tiger mask—made after he saw a photograph in *National Geographic* while on a flight—that has been named one of the scariest designs ever.

The nicknames didn't refer to the mask, but some of Gratton's unusual tales and lifestyle.

A persistent pain in his left side, he said, had been the result of a lance wound during the Inquisition.

"I've seen it in my mind. Was I a knight? No, just a simple soldier," he told *The Hockey News* in 1977. "But I was killed when I was run through with a lance."

He also claimed, in an interview with Marv Albert, that in a previous life he helped stone people to death.

"In my last life I was a Spanish Count," he said, "and one of the things I loved to do when I was a count in Spain was take all the commoners, line them up against a wall, and throw rocks at them."

Playing goal and facing pucks nightly was his punishment for past sins, he said.

"He was a piece of work," former road roommate John Davidson recalled, referring to Gratton's musical skills, the time he refused to play because the moon was in the wrong place in the sky, and his tendency to hang out naked after practice.

Gratton didn't just fall from the heavens. A very good minor-league goalie, Gratton had played in the World Hockey Association for three years, leaving with a solid 81-66-7 record (with 4 shutouts and a 3.69 GAA) in 161 games. He also played briefly for the St. Louis Blues, before joining the Rangers as an unrestricted free agent, and walked away from hockey at age 24. He was 11-18-7 with a 4.22 goals-against-average in those 41 games for the Rangers.

In 2006, he told the *New York Times* that he had spent three years at ashrams in India and the next 20 or so moving around Europe before returning to Quebec.

In the story, Gratton recalled playing in an era without goalie coaches or sports psychologists. "Being left alone, not knowing what to do, a lot of us went off the deep end," he said. "I guess I was the weirdest of all. I think I did it just to put the pressure off."

9 An outstanding executive who was inducted into the Hockey Hall of Fame in 1997 as the architect of five Stanley Cups in Edmonton, Sather had begun his minor-league playing career with the Edmonton Oil Kings in 1961 and continued in the NHL with the Bruins and Penguins.

On January 6, 1971, general manager and head coach Emile Francis acquired Sather, then a 27-year-old left wing, from Pittsburgh for Syl Apps Jr. and Sheldon Kannegiesser.

In the days of the GAG trio, Sather was a lower line agitator who played 186 regular-season and 38 playoff games for

New York with 18 goals and 24 assists before he was traded to the St. Louis Blues in 1973. His playing career ended in Edmonton, then of the World Hockey Association (WHA), in 1976–77.

Meanwhile. Apps became one of the Penguins' first stars. Between 1973 and 1976, he centered the Century Line with left wing Lowell MacDonald and right wing Jean Pronovost and led the team in scoring three times.

After 25 years with the Oilers, Sather resigned as general manager and president in 2000, citing irreconcilable differences with the ownership group. "When you got a collection of 37 people with different personalities and different goals, changes are going to happen," he explained. "It doesn't mean that somebody's right or somebody's wrong, it just means it's time to part ways."

So, the Alberta native returned to New York as president and general manager.

Although Sather was always willing to spend in order to give the Rangers opportunities to raise the Cup, and since 2006, his clubs made the playoffs every season but one, his best efforts came up short.

In his tenure, the drafts—given the team's position in the pecking order—have been good, although there have been doozies. In 2003, the choice of Hugh Jessiman at No. 12 stands out in what was a deep pool. Of the 30 players chosen in a first round that included Zach Parise, Ryan Getzlaf, Corey Perry, and Mike Richards, who were still on available at 12, Jessiman only played two NHL games.

Some of the big dollars spent on free agents went to waste also. Three examples: Bobby Holik (five years at $45 million, buyout after two), Scott Gomez (seven years, $49 million, 128 points in two seasons, then traded to Montreal), and defenseman Wade Redden, at 31 (six years, $39 million).

And Sather never really excelled as coach: when he stepped behind the Rangers bench as an interim coach in 2002–03 and 2003–04, he was 33-39-11-7 in 90 games.

10 Known as Rexi, Reijo Ruotsalainen was a steal in the sixth round of the 1980 draft after starring for Karpat Oulu in Finland's Elite League. In that great 1984–85 season, when he was 24, the smallish (5-8, 170 pounds) son of a coach had 73 points, tied for ninth in team history by a defenseman.

As a youngster in Finland, Ruotsalainen's stature forced him to be a goalie and he couldn't afford skates, so the story goes that he stood between the posts in felt boots. He became a blueliner at age 14.

When he arrived in New York in 1981 and spoke little English, the puck-carrying defenseman with a rocket shot from the blueline was paired with stay-at-homer Barry Beck and scored 18 goals and 56 points. Fans who watched him often called him "Plexi-Rexi" when his wayward one-timers hit the glass behind the net.

By 1984–85, he was often skating on a forward line, but it didn't matter where Rexi played: He averaged a fraction under 20 goals a year (99 in 389 games) and added 11 more in 43 playoff matches. He also had 217 assists, which translated to almost a point-a-game pace.

Ruotsalainen was part of a multi-player deal with Edmonton in March 1987, where he won two Cups, in 1987 and 1990.

Speedy defenseman Reijo Ruotsalainen, shown battling future teammate Wayne Gretzky for the puck on Nov. 17, 1985, had scored 73 points in 80 games in his previous season with New York to lead the Rangers in scoring. He would later win two Stanley Cups with Gretzky and the Edmonton Oilers. (AP Photo/Ray Stubblebine)

11 1951.

The NHL required all teams to have a dark home jersey and a light away jersey. Due to the increasing number of newsreels, the league wanted contrasting color to distinguish the teams.

"RANGERS" was arranged diagonally, in blue with a red shadow. Blue, white, and red stripes circled the bottom and sleeves, with a blue shoulder yoke and thin white and red stripes. The whites have remained virtually unchanged.

The Rangers had tinkered with the initial sweater—blue with white striping—in the 1940s, and in 1946, hoping to reverse their losing ways, added a number to the front of the jersey. When they missed the playoffs, they reverted to the familiar uniform.

In 1963, shoulder numbers and the string-tie collar were added, then in 1970, the color scheme changed back to white at home and blue for the road, a pattern that stayed until 2003. Hockey Night in Canada had suggested that the home team wear white jerseys in order to better display the visiting team's more colorful array of away jerseys.

In 2003, it was back to blue at home and white on the road. During the late 1990s, teams had begun to wear and sell alternate "third" jerseys. The Rangers' Miss Liberty design was born, for instance, and in later seasons, new jerseys were designed for special occasions and outdoor games.

12 On March 21, 1994, the Rangers were atop the NHL standings, but their lead over the Devils was down to a point. It was then that they acquired Stephane Matteau, Brian Noonan, Glenn Anderson, and Craig MacTavish in three separate trades prior to the NHL trade deadline. Mike Keenan, who had general manager Neil Smith's ear, wanted more grit. Knowing that Smith wasn't at all averse to trades, especially late in the season, Keenen took advantage, saying: "I believed in deadline deals, to change your team, to tweak it for the playoffs. I don't believe that the same team that wins in an 82-game schedule wins in a 16-win schedule."

Keenan admired the feisty, 6-foot-4 Matteau, 24, who was playing for the Blackhawks. Hawks GM Bob Pulford wanted Tony Amonte and Smith wrangled Brian Noonan, 28, as well. Smith then sought a checking center for depth and turned to Oilers GM Glen Sather, who he had been speaking with for some time as the Oilers played their way out of a playoff spot. He asked for Craig MacTavish, a third liner who could win faceoffs and help on the penalty kill. He also had played with Messier and Graves in Edmonton and sent Todd Marchant west.

Keenan wanted more grit than goals from Gartner, 34, who had scored 40 goals nine times. Smith spoke to Toronto GM Cliff Fletcher and offered the scorer for Glenn Anderson, whose contract was up at the end of the season; Gartner had another year. Twelve games were left in the season, and the Rangers went 8-2-2.

After running roughshod over the Islanders and Capitals, the four paid dividends. Matteau became the hero of the Devils series when he scored two double-overtime goals; the second, in Game 7, lifted the Rangers into the Final against the Vancouver Canucks, where Anderson had back-to-back winning goals in Games 2 and 3. MacTavish assisted on the winning goal in Game 4, and Noonan had an assist on Messier's second-period goal in Game 7 that proved to be the Cup winner.

13 The Toronto St. Patricks.

On November 20, 1926, just four days after the first home opener, the Rangers defeated the St. Patricks, 5-1, as captain Bill Cook recorded the first hat trick in franchise history. The St. Patricks had won the Stanley Cup in 1922, but were in and out of financial trouble, and were sold on February 14, 1927, for $160,000 to Conn Smythe and renamed the Maple Leafs. They finished the season with the new name.

The first home game at the Garden? On November 16, in front of more than 13,000 fans, the Rangers beat the Montreal Maroons 1-0 on Bill Cook's goal at 18:37 of the second period.

14 New York City Mayor Rudolph Giuliani.

First, let's step back for a minute to review just how the name "Mr. October" stuck to Yankees slugger Reggie Jackson.

Yankees catcher Thurman Munson, who didn't get along with Jackson (formerly a star and clutch hitter during his years with the Oakland A's), was being interviewed during the 1977 World Series, which pitted the Bronx Bombers against the Dodgers.

Munson suggested that Jackson, because of his past postseason performances, might be the better interview. "Go ask Mister October," he sneered.

Well, Jackson hit home runs in Games 4 and 5 of the Series and three in the Series-clinching Game 6, each on the first pitch, off three Dodgers pitchers.

So, decades later, here came Messier, whose accomplishments with the Oilers dynasty were legendary. And now he had brought the Stanley Cup back to New York after 54 years.

He was already known as "Moose," "The Messiah," and simply, "The Captain," but on an 89-degree day with shredded computer paper drifting from windows along the Canyon of Heroes in downtown Manhattan, it was New York City Mayor Rudolph Giuliani, who was a huge Yankees fan, that made him a calendar boy on that day.

15 Troy Mallette, 305.

For two seasons, in 1989–90 (as a rookie) and 1990–91, Mallette could have rented space in the sin bin, spending 305 minutes and 252 minutes, respectively, off the ice. They rank as two of the top three in minutes, in Rangers history, separated by Kris King's 286 in 1989–90.

Like a comet, Mallette crashed through the hockey universe for two seasons on Broadway. He was 19 when he set the all-time record for penalty minutes in a season.

A second-round draft pick of the Rangers in 1988 (22nd overall), Mallette changed his style to fit his new team.

"When I went to [training] camp I read the papers just like anyone else, and saw that [the Rangers] needed a physical

Tough left wing Troy Mallette got started early in the 1989–90 season, during which he set the franchise record for penalty minutes with 305 in 79 games. He scrapped with Devils defenseman Ken Daneyko during an exhibition game at the Garden, Sept. 21, 1989. (AP Photo/Ron Frehm)

left winger. I came out of junior as a center who could put up points, but they had that position filled, so I basically turned myself into what the Rangers needed," he later told the Rangers website.

Because of his fearlessness, he rode shotgun on the left side of scorers Bernie Nicholls and Mike Gartner.

Mallette was a very popular rough-and-tumble player over his two seasons. It was Mallette's crushing, illegal check in the third game of the Patrick Division semifinal series against the Islanders in 1990 that left Jeff Norton unconscious and out of the fourth game.

But he also will be remembered, in an odd way, for how his time with the organization ended.

In the summer of 1991, he was shipped to the Edmonton Oilers as compensation for New York signing a free agent: Adam Graves, the heart-and-soul Blueshirt who would help the Rangers win the Stanley Cup in 1994 and whose No. 9 hangs from the rafters at Madison Square Garden.

Mallette left his mark with the Blueshirt Faithful, though, racking up the fights to go along with 13 goals, 16 assists, and 29 points over 79 games, and then continuing with 12 goals, 22 points, and 252 penalty minutes in his second season.

"I was a little bit jealous [after being shipped to Edmonton], obviously being compensation for Adam Graves, and then he's such a big part of that Stanley Cup win. I look back and probably couldn't have scored like he did, but I like to think I could have been a piece somewhere else on that team if things had been different . . . Edmonton had no plans for me and they were disappointed with who they got for Graves."

Part II: Here's the ranking of the players who collected the most career penalty minutes for the Rangers:

Ron Greschner 1,226

Jeff Beukeboom 1,157

Harry Howell 1,147

Dave Maloney 1,113

Vic Hadfield 1,036 (The only forward in the top 5)

Nick Fotiu 970

Lou Fontinato 939

Adam Graves 810

Ching Johnson 798

Barry Beck 775

Jim Neilson 766

Don Maloney 739

For many fans, most of the names on this list were among their favorite players. Nick Fotiu, the Staten Islander and a former amateur boxer who travelled by bus and subway to learn to skate and eventually reached his dream, but never forgot his roots, was one.

Then there was Tie Domi, just below this group, a flat-out brawler with an astounding 526 minutes in penalties in 82 games over three seasons, from 1990–91 to 1992–93. That's an average of more than six minutes per game.

In interviews about his book, Domi, who played for the Winnipeg Jets and Toronto Maple Leafs for 14 years after leaving New York and complied a total of 3,515 penalty minutes and another 238 in the playoffs, tried to explain his violent career.

"There was always a negative, dark cloud over fighting for some reason or another. When I did it, when the Bob Proberts of the world did it, we did it to protect our teammates, and to make people accountable. I think the league is now doing a much better job. But you have to protect your players. The players are the game."

There's another Rangers connection with Domi: Adam Graves.

"We used to live together," Domi recalled, "and we'd wrestle all the time to see who goes to pick up McDonald's. And I can tell you I never lost. I like to rub that in his face. But he is a sweet guy. He is one of the nicest guys you'll ever meet. I kept my sister and my cousin away from hockey players my whole career, but when Adam asked if he could have Violet's phone number to take her to dinner and a show, I said 'yes.' Now he's married to my cousin and they have a beautiful family with three children and I'm a godparent to one of their daughters."

16 Frank Boucher.

Boucher, who was born in Ottawa, centered the Bread Line with brothers Bill and Bun Cook, and together they had quite a run. With the Bread Line, the Rangers won the Stanley Cup in 1928 and 1933 and reached the Finals in 1932. Boucher also was behind the bench for the 1940 championship.

In 533 games, the playmaking Boucher scored 413 points, including 261 assists, and spent almost no time in the penalty box: just 115 minutes. In 55 playoff games, he only had 12 minutes in penalties.

It was that latter talent that became part of his NHL legacy.

In 1925, Lady Byng, the wife of Viscount Byng, the Governor-General of Canada, donated a trophy to be awarded to the league's "most gentlemanly player." Boucher won the hardware seven times in eight years, from 1928 to 1935. In a nod to his accomplishment, she gave him the trophy to keep and donated a second one. No player has won it more times. Wayne Gretzky was presented it five times.

The original was destroyed at a fire at Boucher's house in 1962, but the league had already fashioned a third trophy in her honor after Lady Byng died in 1949.

Boucher had been coaching the New York Rovers, the Rangers minor-league affiliate, then took over the Rangers from Lester Patrick, who retired before the 1939–40 season. Boucher's club finished second with a 27-11-10 record, and ousted the Boston Bruins in six games to advance to the Finals. The Rangers won the first two games at home, but because the circus had set up shop at Madison Square Garden, a common occurrence in that era, the series shifted to Toronto, where they lost twice to the Leafs. Muzz Patrick's overtime goal won Game 5, 2-1, and Bryan Hextall's overtime goal, just 2:33 into the extra session of Game 6, sealed the franchise's third Cup, with a 3-2 decision.

Boucher was the sixth rookie coach to win the Cup, and he and Lester Patrick became the first duo to win the championship trophy together as players and as a coach-manager pair.

In the 1945–46 season—after Boucher had come of out retirement at age 42 to play 15 games in the 1943–44 season with the roster decimated by the military draft—Boucher, then coach, began alternating Chuck Rayner and "Sugar" Jim Henry (who loved brown sugar, especially on cereal) every game, sometimes after periods, which hadn't been done previously, and occasionally on shifts.

"We weren't crazy about the system," Rayner once said. "But we were roommates and best friends, so we lived with it."

Coach Frank Boucher (second from right), in this practice at Ice-
land Rink on Broadway and 53rd Street in Manhattan on October
28, 1947, with defenseman Frank Eddolls, center Buddy O'Connor
and defenseman Fred Shero, was one of the greatest Rangers in
history. He starred on the 1928 and 1933 Stanley Cup winners and
coached the club during its third championship season in 1940.
(AP Photo/John Rooney)

Rayner was one of the first butterfly-style goalies and mas-
tered the poke check to knock the puck away from attackers.
He won the Hart Trophy as NHL MVP in 1950.

But that was in the beginning of a dark era for the franchise: the Rangers made the playoffs just twice between 1943
and 1956, and then just once from 1959 to 1966 before a nine-
year string of success.

Boucher was not forgotten, though. He was inducted into
the Hockey Hall of Fame in 1958.

17 The common thread here is the chant of "19-40" that rose like a dark thundercloud in buildings like the Nassau Coliseum and the Meadowlands Arena, where the Islanders and Devils called home, and where home fans tried to taunt the poor Rangers fans who had gone through a horrendous drought. After all, both the Islanders and Devils had won Cups in the interim: four from 1980 to 1983 for the Islanders and three (1995, 2000, and 2003) for the Devils. The chant was their weapon a half-century later, after the 1940 Cup.

In 1941, the year following the third Cup for the Blueshirts, the mortgage on the 15-year-old Madison Square Garden, which had replaced the one on East 26th Street and Madison Avenue at the turn of the century, had been paid off.

In a very visible display of glee, management burned the document in the bowl of the prestigious silver trophy, which many considered the Holy Grail of the Canadian sport. In their minds, the hockey gods would punish the New Yorkers for the desecration.

But the more public, and accepted, version of the story is known as "Dutton's Curse."

This explanation comes from the rival New York Americans, a Madison Square Garden co-tenant and the first team to play there.

Once entrepreneur "Tex" Rickard saw that hockey could be successful in the building that was built around boxing, he acquired the rights to another NHL team, which became the Rangers. Without the corporation's financial support and marketing, which shifted to the new club, the Americans foundered. In 1937, the league assumed ownership of the Americans, or "Amerks," as they were known, and they actually beat the

Rangers in the playoffs that season, but lost to the Chicago Blackhawks in the semifinals.

Nonetheless, a wound had been opened, and World War II caused much more bleeding.

The Americans lost almost all their players to military service and the league decided to fold the franchise after the 1941 season.

"Red" Dutton, the Americans' owner, blamed the Rangers hierarchy for encouraging NHL executives to kill the internal competition in the city and vowed that the franchise would never win a championship in his lifetime.

Norman Alexander Dutton was born in Winnipeg and played as a battling defenseman for five years for the Calgary Tigers of the Western Hockey League, leading the club in penalty minutes each year. His rights were sold to the NHL's Montreal Maroons in 1926, and he played there for four seasons. He was sold to the New York Americans in a multi-player deal in 1930, and here's where our tale starts.

Dutton continued his aggressive play and was popular with his teammates, but the Americans failed to make the playoffs for four of his first five seasons. He was named coach in the 1935–36 season, and became the second player-coach in NHL history.

It didn't really help, and when the curtain fell, Dutton remained bitter. He thought if the Americans could have survived during the global conflict, "we would have run the Rangers right out of the rink," he said.

But following the death of Frank Calder in 1943, Dutton agreed to serve as acting president of the league and arranged financing for an arena in Brooklyn in 1946, but the league's board wasn't interested. Angered, he didn't attend an NHL

Ending a 54-year drought and vanquishing two mythical curses on the storied franchise, Rangers players raised the Stanley Cup during a parade on June 17, 1994, as about a million fans lined lower Broadway's "Canyon of Heroes." Presidents, prime ministers, US astronauts, and Yankees and Mets championships teams were similarly honored. (AP Photo/Justin Sutcliffe)

game until 1980, for a ceremony honoring the Calgary Tigers. His business interests continued: he invested in the Calgary Stampeders, the Canadian Football League team, and was named president.

Dutton died in 1987. Seven years later, the Rangers finally won the Cup.

Those are facts. But if you're superstitious, you might believe in Dutton's Curse.

18 Hardy Astrom. The Swedish goalkeeper made 29 saves at the Montreal Forum in a 6-3 Rangers win on February 28.

A 26-year-old third-stringer, Astrom was tabbed by coach John Ferguson to go between the pipes against a team that was gliding through the league. "When you go to Montreal, you'll try anything," Ferguson said.

Astrom, who won a silver medal with Team Sweden in the 1977 World Cup, put on a brave face. "I had played big games before with Sweden. I had beaten the Russians in Moscow and the Czechs in Prague," he said.

Steve Vickers scored the opening goal and Phil Esposito followed up with a tip-in, and the Blueshirts were up 2-0 in the first period before Jacques Lemaire scored. Eddie Johnstone and Don Murdoch extended the lead to 4-0 and Ron Duguay and Mark Heaslip had the Canadiens on the rocks. Two late goals made the score a little more respectable.

Needless to say, the Rangers were overjoyed. "Fergie bought a blow-up Stanley Cup and we carried it on the bus and the plane home," defenseman Dave Maloney recalled.

Astrom's career went downhill after that, though. He went 1-2 with a 3.50 GAA, and was traded to Colorado in July 1979.

Then-Rockies coach Don Cherry wasn't impressed.

"First practice, we were working on breakout drills, I shoot the puck at Hardy from the far blue line, and it goes right through his legs. 'Fluke,' I figure, so I shoot another. Right through the legs again. 'Next drill,' I said . . . . Actually Hardy was a nice guy, he just had a weakness with pucks."

19 The first telecast of an NHL game was in 1940. The first nationally televised game was in 1957. And the Rangers hosted both at Madison Square Garden.

To be sure, in 1940, it wasn't exactly *Hockey Night in America*, with colorful graphics, multiple cameras, instant replays, cut-ins to other games, electronic noises, and all the other bells and whistles of today's coverage of the NHL.

Instead, when the Rangers hosted the Montreal Canadiens at Madison Square Garden on February 25, 1940, there was one camera, in a fixed position. The game aired on station W2XBS, an experimental (non-commercial) station in New York and could be seen on 300 small television receivers in New York, mostly in the homes of television executives and engineers.

Those who watched saw the Blueshirts prevail, 6-2, for their 14th straight home victory.

Hockey was in good company for the fledgling industry. When the Empire State Building was completed in 1931, RCA leased the 85th floor for a studio and transmitter location for its broadcasting division, NBC. By 1939, most of the W2XBS broadcasts were live from the New York World's Fair, including President Franklin D. Roosevelt's opening speech. In 1939, it carried the first live telecasts of Major League Baseball and the NFL. Then in 1940, it carried the first college hoops game—Fordham hosting the University of Pittsburgh at the

Garden—the Metropolitan Opera, and the 1940 Republican National Convention in Philadelphia.

Seventeen years later, on the afternoon of January 5, 1957, the Rangers hosted the Chicago Black Hawks at 2 p.m., and a much, much larger audience tuned in.

Not only was it the first ever matinee for the Blueshirts at the Garden—with 9,853 fans in attendance, including NHL Commissioner Clarence Campbell—it was the first of 10 coast-to-coast broadcasts by CBS, which had agreed to a one-year contract with the NHL. More than 100 stations, from Buffalo to Los Angeles, carried the game, with Bud Palmer handling the play-by-play and Fred Cusick the commentary.

The game was close until late, when Rangers right wing Bruce Cline and left wing Danny Lewicki scored 20 seconds apart. Without a doubt, television and the Rangers started as a good pairing. The Blueshirts won again, 4-1.

20 John Davidson unknowingly, and unexpectedly, birthed a rock and roll chart-topper in 1978.

In a playoff game on April 13 at Madison Square Garden, a Buffalo player rang a shot off Davidson's mask and he shook his head, trying to clear his sight and shake off the cobwebs.

"I got my bell rung pretty good," said Davidson.

Lou Gramm and members of the band—who were Sabres fans—were in the studio and heard Jim Gordon and Bill Chadwick repeatedly mention the phrase "Double Vision."

The band was stuck on one particular track and as Davidson was helped off the ice, Gramm recalled, "[The announcer] said he was going to be all right, but that he had been experiencing some double vision. Voila! A siren went off in my head. Double Vision. Perfect."

Goalie John Davidson stopped pucks however he could and ducked to avoid the rest, as he did in this 3-1 win over the Islanders in a semifinal playoff game at the Garden on May 1, 1979. The season prior, a song penned after J.D. was shaken by a shot off his mask became a rock hit. (AP Photo/Ray Stubblebine)

After writing some lyrics, Gramm said he "told Mick [Jones] and the guys that I had solved our problem. They looked at me like I was crazy at first, but after I told them about double vision and began singing some of the lyrics, they were excited too—so excited that we wound up making it the title track."

"Double Vision" was a smash and the album sold six million copies.

Unlike Foreigner, the Rangers didn't strike it so rich. They won that game 4-3 but lost the next one and the series.

Songwriters could have generated many ideas if they listened to Chadwick, the color analyst to Jim Gordon's play-by-play known as "The Big Whistle" and the NHL's first American-born linesman and referee.

Chadwick had begun officiating in 1939, four years after suffering an injury in the minors that cost him most of the sight in his right eye. He worked until 1955, and to avoid keeping his hands in his pockets, created hand signals to call a penalty. Many of those same signals remain in use today. When he retired at age 39, he said: "If you wait until they ask you to leave, it's too late."

From 1967 through 1981, Chadwick, who grew up on 122nd Street and Second Avenue in Manhattan, spent four years on the radio with Marv Albert and 11 with Gordon on Channel 9.

Imagine some of these song titles. . . .

Chadwick's "Shoot the puck, Barry," an exhortation to the hulking defenseman's reluctance to launch the pill at the net, and in his hurry to react, often stumbled comically: "Great save, off his left-hand foot."

In some ways, he was hockey's version of Phil Rizzuto, who could turn a phrase without the cannoli. The Big Whistle once remarked on the air that Rangers center Gene Carr "couldn't put the puck in the ocean if he was standing on the pier."

After Carr was shipped to the California Golden Seals, he scored in a road game against the Rangers. Gordon didn't miss the opening. "I thought you said Carr couldn't put the puck in the ocean," he said.

"Well Jim," Chadwick quickly responded, "it's a bigger ocean out here."

21 In his second season, Henrik Lundqvist played against his identical twin brother, Joel, for the first time and made 43 saves as the Rangers defeated the Dallas Stars, 5-2, in Dallas.

Joel Lundqvist was called up from Iowa of the AHL after Stars center Mike Modano was placed on injured reserve.

Identical twins Henrik and Joel Lundqvist faced each other on NHL ice several times, including at the Garden (above) on Oct. 20, 2008, when the Rangers hosted the Stars. The first time they met in the NHL was in Dallas on Dec. 15, 2006. They joined forces on Team Sweden to win the gold medal in the IIHF World Championships in May 2017. (AP Photo/Kathy Willens)

Joel, who is 40 minutes younger, played only 5:44 and didn't take a shot in his fifth NHL game.

"I never see players out there but I noticed every time he was on the ice," Henrik said. "I was nervous every time he was out there. Getting the chance to play against him in the NHL is a special feeling."

It was the third matchup of twins in NHL history. Rich and Ron Sutter were the last set to meet up on March 14, 1994. Patrik and Peter Sundstrom played against each other 18 times.

During one practice when they were eight or nine, the coach asked if anyone wanted to be a goaltender. Joel grabbed and raised Henrik's arm and said that his brother would like to.

When you think of it, that was the first step in of one of the most remarkable careers in Rangers history, which began in the small town of Are, population 1,500, and continued in Sweden with the Frolunda Indians, starting at age 16.

The dashing goalie, who was once featured in a *New York Times* article as "Hockey's God of Fashion," is much more substance than style.

His stats tell the story.

Consider:

Since making his debut in 2005–06, The King—called Hank by his teammates—leads all NHL goalies (with a minimum of 400 appearances) in games played, wins, and shutouts, ranks second in goals-against-average, and is tied for second in save percentage. He won the Vezina Trophy in the 2011–12 season and is a five-time finalist for the award. He also has the most wins by a European-born goalie in league history.

Lundqvist, who turned 35 in 2017, leads all active goaltenders in playoff appearances, wins, and shutouts.

He became the first goalie to record at least 20 wins in each of his first 12 seasons and one of three goalies (along with Martin Brodeur and Patrick Roy) to have at least 11 seasons of 30 or more wins.

Lundqvist, a guitar player and collector and tennis player who is a friend of Roger Federer, also won a gold medal playing for Team Sweden in the 2006 Olympics.

A list of his accomplishments covers multiple pages. Among the Rangers records he holds are: wins, appearances, shutouts, saves, minutes played, save percentage, playoff wins, playoff shutouts, playoff save percentage, shootout wins, wins by a rookie, and on and on. He was named team MVP for eight of his 12 seasons.

The two words he speaks the most when describing his game are focus and mindset. Players and coaches say he has an extraordinary ability to concentrate yet also let his reflexes take over.

After games, he can recount exactly what happened on a big save or a goal, and dissect the play.

When the Rangers clinched the first-round series against the Montreal Canadiens last April in the sixth game at Madison Square Garden, for instance, he made a stop on forward Tomas Plekanec in the waning minutes that preserved a one-goal lead.

"I knew I was in trouble because I wasn't in position on the first play and then he threw the puck at me. My first thought was, 'Don't knock it in,' and then it ends up right on his stick," he said in the jammed locker room afterward. "It was just a desperation save. Luckily, he didn't put it far corner. It was just a quick play. I knew with two minutes to go, it was going to be one or two more saves and if I could come up with those, we were going to be in good shape."

Or how about this comment after a loss to the Canadiens on February 21, 2017, discussing defenseman Shea Weber's heavy shot?

"There are a couple guys in the league that when they shoot, it's almost like you have to make two saves, because you think you have it and it just keeps going," he said. "It's like a drill and it just keeps going through your arm and your armpit. You think you have it under control but it always surprises you, how hard it is. Obviously, I want it back, but at the same time, it's much harder than anyone else. Next time, I'll try to get the body behind it instead of just the arm."

And although he doesn't wear the "C," Lundqvist thrives on pressure and leads by example, and players listen.

After the Rangers fell behind two games to one against Montreal in the opening round of the playoffs in April 2017, he bluntly explained what was needed from the team.

"It's important we start with ourselves," he said. "We need more, it's as simple as that. I didn't come up with the saves on the penalty kill. We all need to be better. Our power play did not get going and get any momentum for us. Every little detail matters in this game. Every play. We are going to need our best from everyone and from myself. That's the only way for us to win the next game."

Teammates have run out of superlatives over the years.

"He's one of the top five goalies in the world," said Ryan McDonagh. "He's just so consistent in his preparation and continues to be super competitive in practice and that carries over to his games. He's someone who has a lot of care and passion for the sport, this organization, and this city."

On the personal side, the unquestioned face of the franchise has settled down. He and his wife have two daughters, who live in Manhattan and return to Sweden in the summer. But the intensity on the ice, and even in practice, where he hates to allow a goal, never wanes.

When he stopped 54 shots against the Canadiens in another first-round game of the 2017 playoffs that the Rangers lost in overtime, writers scrambled to check the all-time team record. It is one of the ones that Lundqvist doesn't own: Mike Richter stopped 59 shots in Vancouver on January 31, 1991, in a 3-3 tie.

Beyond the strong will to win and the unsurpassable work ethic, Lundqvist has a not-so-secret weapon: Benoit Allaire.

After Lundqvist passed his boyhood idol, Hall of Famer Dominik Hasek, with his 390th win, in Denver on December 31, 2016, to become the winningest European-born goaltender in NHL history, he praised the easygoing goalie coach who has been a mentor and friend since his rookie season.

"I think the most important person for me, ever since I got here, was Benoit Allaire," Lundqvist said. "To have the consistency, to have a guy that is so positive and so much structure in the way he works—it's just been great to get to know him a little bit. He knows me really well, how I work, how I feel. It's just fun to come to work." From on-ice tutoring to reviewing video, Lundqvist said that the two have never had a major disagreement.

In New York, Allaire, 55, has not only tutored Lundqvist, but raised the level of Cam Talbot (who started 73 games to help the Edmonton Oilers reach the playoffs in 2016–17 after being traded from the Rangers) as well as backup Antti Raanta.

Prior to 2004, during seven years in Phoenix, the Quebec native who runs a goalie school with his brother Francois oversaw a rebirth of veteran Sean Burke and changed the style of Brian Boucher, who holds the current-day NHL shutout record of 332:01.

To end the Lundqvist question, here's one more bit of "Did you know" scoop.

Two years before Lundqvist was drafted, the Rangers actually picked another Lundqvist.

Stefan Lundqvist, a right wing, played three seasons in the Swedish Elite League for Brynäs IF after he was drafted 180th overall in 1998. He never played in the NHL.

As it turned out, the second Lundqvist pick was the charm.

22 Don Murdoch and Mark Pavelich.

Murdoch tallied five on the road against Gary "Suitcase" Smith in a 10-4 victory over the Minnesota North Stars on October 12, 1976. Simply put, Murdoch was a sniper. As a 20-year-old rookie, Murdoch, who had played in Medicine Hat, scored 56 points in 59 games his rookie season, including a Rangers rookie record of 32 goals.

But Murdoch's off-ice issues derailed a promising career.

In the summer of 1977, Murdoch was nabbed by customs agents in Toronto with 4.5 grams of cocaine hidden in his socks. He was suspended for the entire 1978–79 season (a penalty later reduced to 40 games) and admitted to having drinking and drug problems. In 1980-1981, he did set a club record for most single-season game-winning goals—nine—which would later be tied by Mark Messier (1996–97) and Jaromir Jagr (2005–06).

Pavelich, who was not drafted, scored the quintet at home against Hartford's Greg Millen in an 11-3 win on February 23, 1983. It was three years to the day that the 1980 United States

Olympic team, of which Pavs was a part, won the gold medal at Lake Placid, the event known as the "Miracle on Ice." He was the first American to score five goals in an NHL game.

"We want six! We want six!," the crowd chanted after Pavelich's fifth goal with 11:09 seconds left in the third period at Madison Square Garden.

When Pavelich, 24, scored the hat trick in the second period, hundreds of identical red baseball caps, handed out as part of a cigarette company promotion, sailed to the ice from the stands.

THIRD PERIOD

If you want to win any game in regulation, the third period is the key. Like the fourth quarter in football or basketball, or the ninth inning in baseball, as they say, it's not how you start, it's how you finish.

But it's not at all easy. Every squad wants the two points for a regulation victory. The intensity level rises and any mistake can be turned into a win—or a loss.

1 A double-stumper: Only once have the Rangers had the No. 1 overall pick in the NHL draft. Who was he? And who was the first player ever drafted by the Blueshirts? *Answer on page 123.*

2 Who leads the Rangers in all-time playoff games? Hint: He was an undrafted defenseman. *Answer on page 129.*

3 Without a doubt, current fans recognize Dan Girardi as the team's ironman. But who holds the amazing record for consecutive games played? *Answer on page 131.*

4 Gordie Howe, Joe Sakic, Ziggy Palffy, Steven Stamkos. Which of these players was close to becoming a Ranger? *Answer on page 132.*

5 He scored just four goals as a Ranger. Half of them came in the 2012 Winter Classic in Philadelphia, and his celebration afterward triggered some controversy. Who is this winger-turned-TV analyst? *Answer on page 134.*

6 Speaking of outdoor games, how many have the Rangers played? *Answer on page 136.*

7 Which coach had the shortest post-game "press conference" of the 2011–12 season—and one of the briefest of all time—16 seconds? *Answer on page 138.*

8 Hall of Fame goalie Terry Sawchuk played for the Rangers just before his career ended in avoidable circumstances after a fight with another player. Who was that player? *Answer on page 140.*

9 Which team have the Rangers played the most playoff games against, and who have the Rangers beaten the most in playoff series? And what about the regular season? *Answer on page 141.*

10 Who has been the most proficient player in shootouts for the Rangers? *Answer on page 141.*

11 In order to obtain a long-time jersey number when coming to a new team, players often ask the teammate currently wearing the number to switch, and sometimes will offer compensation for the change. In July 2007, two newly signed star players wanted to wear No. 23, and it was determined in an unusual manner. Who were the players and how was it decided? *Answer on page 143.*

12 Athletes are creatures of habit and can be very superstitious—going through the same routines, taping sticks a certain way, lacing up the right skate before the left, eating a certain meal at a certain time. But eight Rangers didn't have a problem wearing No. 13. Can you name them? *Answer on page 145.*

13 Frank Boucher was the leading scorer in the 1928 Stanley Cup Final. And general manager Lester Patrick stepped in as a goaltender for part of one game when Lorne Chabot was injured. But who was the lesser-known, unsung hero in that series? Hint: he had played for another team that season. *Answer on page 148.*

14 In the first decade of the franchise, the overwhelming majority of deals were free-agent signings or acquiring players for cash. For example, goalie Hal Winkler was sold to Boston for cash in January 1927. But which players were the principals in the first actual trade? *Answer on page 149.*

15 My first name is Ulf. I was not only the first Swede to play for the Rangers, but the first European-born-and-bred player to skate in the NHL. Who am I? *Answer on page 150.*

16 There are two Chiefs in Rangers lore: one a player and one a fan. Remember? *Answer on page 151.*

17 Which former general manager re-designed the Rangers jerseys with a front shield that was so wildly unpopular with players and fans that they were scrapped after two seasons? *Answer on page 153.*

18 Which opposing player, known as a goon, once "mooned" the Rangers fans at Madison Square Garden after a brawl? *Answer on page 153.*

19 This jumping jack from Guelph, Ontario, said he loved New York for the food and fans. "I like the ravioli and I like the people. They all look like Paisans." Who was he? *Answer on page 154.*

20 Why is Al Dorrington an important figure in Rangers history? *Answer on page 156.*

21 In honor of a unique feat, the hat trick, here's a multi-part question.

Coach Alain Vigneault calls Jesper Fast "Quickie."

This former Rangers wing wasn't as speedy, but he scored on his first NHL shot and later recorded the fastest hat trick in team history—in 2:30. He is _____.

Now, which Ranger scored the first hat trick at home, who leads the franchise in hat tricks, and just how did this turn of phrase become part of the hockey lexicon? *Answer on page 157.*

22 Because scoring is so essential in the third period, which is where we are in this journey, let's move the needle a notch. How many Rangers scored four goals in a game? *Answer on page 167.*

23 We left those speed questions behind, so let's circle back. Who scored the fastest goals at the start of a game? *Answer on page 170.*

24 Head coach Herb Brooks once said that to ask this player to muck in the corners was "like asking Picasso to paint a garage." Yes, he was a talented free spirit with flair. He is _____. *Answer on page 172.*

25 Which Rangers were in the Ooh-La-La Sasson commercials? *Answer on page 174.*

THIRD PERIOD—
ANSWERS

1 The momentous occasion came in the third ever annual amateur draft in 1965. André Veilleux, a right wing out of the Montreal juniors, was the first overall pick. But he never played a game in the NHL.

In that draft, Michel Parizeau, a left wing, was the third pick of the Rangers and later played for the St. Louis Blues, the Philadelphia Flyers, the WHA's Quebec Nordiques, and (get this!) the Indianapolis Racers, including the one season (1978–79) that Wayne Gretzky was there.

And the first player ever selected, back in 1963 at the first amateur draft, was right wing Al Osborne, chosen fourth overall. Osborne was 16 at the time, and played junior hockey in Weston, Ontario. He never did play for the Rangers. He turned pro with the Omaha Knights in 1967 and later played for the Buffalo Bisons (AHL) and the Salem Rebels (EHL).

The first player drafted to actually play for the Rangers was the son of a Hall of Famer—but was quickly traded.

Sylvanus (Syl) Marshall Apps Jr., a center, was drafted 21st overall in 1964. Apps played 31 games in 1970 before he was traded to Pittsburgh—for a winger named Glen Sather—where he blossomed into a star. Between 1973 and 1976, Apps centered the "Century Line" with left wing Lowell MacDonald and right wing Jean Pronovost. He led the team in scoring three times and set a team record in 1972–73 with 85 points, which he then tied in 1973–74. Apps's finest season was 1975–76, when he posted 99 points, on 32 goals and 67 assists.

The Blueshirts were far more fortunate in the 1966 draft.

With the second overall pick, they chose defenseman Brad Park. Since then, they've selected 46 players in the first round, with varying degrees of success.

Here's a complete list of the Rangers' first-round picks over the years—some blue-chippers and some busts.

You deserve a break for getting this far, so take a minute to stroll down memory lane.

1963 Al Osborne (4th overall)
1964 Robert Graham (3rd)
1965 Andre Veilleux (1st)
1966 Brad Park (2nd)
1967 Robert Dickson (6th)
1969 Andre Dupont (8th), Pierre Jarry (12th)
1970 Normand Gratton (11th)
1971 Steve Vickers (10th), Steve Durbano (13th)
1972 Al Blanchard (10th), Bob MacMillan (15th)
1973 Rick Middleton (14th)
1974 Dave Maloney (14th)
1975 Wayne Dillon (12th)
1976 Don Murdoch (6th)
1977 Lucien DeBlois (8th), Ron Duguay (13th)
1979 Doug Sullliman (13th)
1980 Jim Malone (14th)
1981 James Patrick (9th)
1982 Chris Kontos (15th)
1983 Dave Gagner (12th)
1984 Terry Carkner (14th)

1985 Ulf Dahlen (7th)
1986 Brian Leetch (9th)
1987 Jayson More (10th)
1989 Steven Rice (20th)
1990 Michael Stewart (13th)
1991 Alexei Kovalev (15th)
1992 Peter Ferraro (24th)
1993 Niklas Sundstrom (8th)
1994 Dan Cloutier (26th)
1996 Jeff Brown (22nd)
1997 Stefan Cherneski (19th)
1998 Manny Malhotra (7th)
1999 Pavel Brendl (4th), Jamie Lundmark (9th)
2001 Dan Blackburn (10th)
2003 Hugh Jessiman (12th)
2004 Al Montoya (6th), Lauri Korpikoski (19th)
2005 Marc Staal (12th)
2006 Bobby Sanguinetti (21st)
2007 Alexei Cherepanov (17th)
2008 Michael Del Zotto (20th)
2009 Chris Kreider (19th)
2010 Dylan McIlrath (10th)
2011 J.T. Miller (15th)
2012 Brady Skjei (28th)

To be sure, some of the first-rounders developed into absolute gems: Brian Leetch, Alex Kovalev, Rick Middleton, Dave Maloney, Steve Vickers, Ron Duguay, Don Murdoch, Marc Staal, James Patrick, Brad Park.

Sadly, one of the top Rangers prospects in years had his career tragically cut short on a rink in Russia.

At 17, Alexei Cherepanov had more points than predecessors Evgeni Malkin, Alexander Ovechkin, and Ilya Kovalchuk had as rookies in the Russian Super League.

Naturally, scouts were impressed by the skilled, speedy forward from a town just outside Barnaul in southwestern Siberia. But there was some hesitancy when Cherepanov, nicknamed the Siberian Express, became eligible for the NHL draft in 2007. Much of the concern was because there was no transfer agreement between the NHL and the IIHF (International Ice Hockey Federation).

In the first round of the draft, Cherepanov—who had played well for Russia in several international tournaments—slipped out of the top 10 because of the uncertainty. The Rangers grabbed him at 17th and the youngster said he was happy to be selected and hoped he could someday play in New York, "the center of the United States." He attended the Rangers prospect camp, then returned to Avangard Omsk, which had joined the new Kontinental Hockey League (KHL), and had 15 goals in 46 games.

There was a year remaining on his contract with Avangard, which also had Czech superstar Jaromir Jagr on the team that season. On October 13, 2008, in a road game against Vityaz Chekov, Cherepanov skated to the bench after a shift late in the third period, sat next to Jagr, and suddenly collapsed.

Initially, attempts were made to revive Cherepanov on the bench, before he was carried back to the dressing room by his teammates, where doctors worked on him. He was revived briefly, and transferred to a local hospital, where he was pronounced dead later that evening.

It was eventually determined that Cherepanov, then 19, had a heart condition. An investigation also found that the rink's ambulance had left moments earlier and that the defibrillator in the building wasn't working. Two Avangard doctors were banned from the league, one for life, the Vityaz team director also was banned, Avangard's team president was fired, and the league overhauled its emergency response program.

Cherepanov's No. 7 was retired by Avangard, and the Rangers, who had never signed him, were awarded the 17th pick in the second round of the 2009 draft as compensation. Ethan Werek was selected; on May 8, 2011, Werek was traded to the Phoenix Coyotes for Oscar Lindberg.

But there were some high picks that simply didn't pan out.

Take the 1999 draft, when the Rangers had two first-round picks: Pavel Brendl and Jamie Lundmark.

Brendl, a Czech Republic standout, came to North America with the World Hockey League's Calgary Hitmen, where he was moved from center to wing. He made the first All-Star team and piled up the points: 73 goals and 134 points in just 68 games and was the top rookie and league's leading scorer. But he was developing a reputation for being a somewhat lazy player.

In that draft, the consensus was that Brendl, the Sedin Twins (Henrik and Daniel), and Patrik Stefan were the first tier. The Blueshirts spoke with Brendl and were satisfied that he was ready to play in the NHL. So starting goalie Dan Cloutier and some other picks were traded to move up to the fourth spot.

Brendl reported to training camp out of shape, a bad sign. He didn't play defense, shunned advice, and was returned to the Hitmen. He still put up 111 points. He improved in the second camp, but was one of the final cuts. Back in Calgary, he scored 75 points. The Rangers had seen enough, and when center Eric Lindros asked out of Philadelphia, the Rangers sent Brendl to the Flyers. Before long, Brendl ended up in the AHL.

In the 2002–03 season, he did play 42 games with the Flyers, scoring 12 points, and was shipped to the Hurricanes, where he played 26 games over two seasons. Eventually, he played in Sweden and Russia. But he never had what it took to stick in the NHL.

Jamie Lundmark, an Edmonton native, was another highly regarded scorer who never quite made the grade. With the Hartford Wolf Pack in 2001–02, he tied for first among AHL rookies in assists with 32 and scored 27 goals. In 2002–03, he played 55 games with the Rangers, but didn't really impress, with eight goals and 19 points in 55 games, certainly not numbers of a first-rounder.

The following season, he played 56 games and scored just two goals and 10 points. Lundmark bounced around the NHL after that and eventually played for several years in Austria.

Hugh Jessiman, who grew up in Connecticut, was another draftee whose career didn't quite transpire the way the Rangers had planned.

Standing 6-foot-6 and a strapping 224 pounds, Jessiman was nicknamed the Huge Specimen. In his freshman year at Dartmouth, he scored 47 points in 34 games and that summer, was selected ahead of future All-Stars such as Zach Parise, Ryan Getzlaf, Ryan Kesler, Mike Richards, and Corey Perry. Oops.

Jessiman was injured in his sophomore year, and under pressure to live up to the hype, later chose to turn pro and was assigned to the Wolf Pack, where he played for two seasons before being traded and skated with a half-dozen AHL teams.

On a more lighthearted note: there may never have been a more obvious late-round draft pick for the Blueshirts than one that they made during the 1986 draft at the revered Montreal Forum.

With their first selection, the brass had grabbed Brian Leetch. We know how that worked out.

Flash forward rounds later, and the clock was ticking on another Rangers pick, No. 198, in the 10th round.

A 6-foot-4, 225-pound defenseman from Sudbury, Ontario—the hometown of Eddie Shack and Eddie Giacomin—was available. His first name wasn't Eddie, but his last name was Ranger.

Joe Ranger played one season for the Rangers—the Kitchener Rangers of the Ontario Hockey League, in 1987–88, that is. He never pulled on the NHL sweater.

2 Dan Girardi, with 122 postseason games under his belt after the 2016–17 season, is the franchise leader in playoff appearances.

Girardi, who was undrafted in 2003, has made front offices regret that lapse in judgment.

After signing a two-way deal with the Rangers, the Welland, Ontario, native was called up from the AHL on January 27, 2007, after an injury to Darius Kasparaitis, and has been almost impossible to remove from the lineup.

The 33-year-old ironman who consistently ranked among the team's leaders in blocked shots and also hits by a defenseman finished the 2016–17 season ranked ninth on the team's all-time games played list at 788. Only four defensemen have played more: Harry Howell, Jim Neilson, Ron Greschner, and Brian Leetch.

Since 2007, Girardi has played through numerous injuries to appear in 80 or more games in each full (non-lockout) season and 74 in 2015–16.

Last season, the alternate captain—popular with teammates for his tenacity, courage, and sense of humor—missed his longest stretch of time in a decade after being shut down with a severe ankle wound suffered from a blocked shot on February 7. Yet he remained second on the team, and top 20 in the league, in the category of playoff appearances.

In a testament to how successful the team has been in the past decade, only two other current players appear to have a chance to ever catch the battered Girardi, who was bought out of the final three years of his contract in June 2017: Marc Staal has 104 postseason games and Ryan McDonagh, 96. Derek Stepan (97) had also been close, but like Girardi, Stepan was part of the surprising remake of the evolving Rangers last summer. He and goaltender Antti Raanta were traded to Arizona and star defenseman Kevin Shattenkirk was signed as a free agent.

Since the 200–08 season, Girardi—who has played the most games by an undrafted defenseman in team history (788)—leads the NHL in blocked shots, and in the 201–17 season was tied for second in blocked shots per game, and was tied for ninth overall in the league with 166.

Not bad for a guy whose first job was as a dishwasher in Kimono's Chinese Buffet and Restaurant in Welland, Ontario. Girardi, whose idols were former Leafs forward Wendel Clark and Mark Messier, decided to concentrate on hockey in high school, but otherwise says he would have tried to make it as a first baseman in pro baseball.

On warm days in April or September outside the team's training center in Westchester County, when Chris Drury and

Dom Moore were teammates, the three would break out their mitts and toss a baseball around.

"Half the time, I don't understand how he does what he does," said Derek Stepan, who joked about rumors that Girardi, nicknamed G-Money, might actually be a cyborg. "He's able to block shots at all points and still be fine. His body takes a beating at times, and he just always is happy-go-lucky about it."

His willingness to stay in the locker room after wins or losses to talk with the media shows another side of his personality. Girardi gets it.

3 Andy Hebenton.

If you include his 22 playoff games, Hebenton played in 582 straight games for the Blueshirts from 1955–56 to 1962–63 and continued that run with 70 more regular-season games in Boston in 1963–64.

The closest that the 5-foot-9, 185-pound left wing known as "Spud" (due to his passion for potatoes) ever came to missing a game was in 1957, the year in which he won the Lady Byng Memorial Trophy for being the league's most gentlemanly player.

In a game at Madison Square Garden, Hebenton caught a stick in the eye. Afterward, the lid started to puff up. "It shut so tight I couldn't see at all," Hebenton remembered, "but somehow our club doctor managed to squeeze drops of some kind into it the next night in Montreal. The eye opened up a little—just enough so that I could get into the game."

Hebenton, a concrete worker in the offseason, proved to be much more than a warrior and mucker after the Rangers brought him up from Victoria of the Western League in 1955. In his rookie season, he led the team with 24 goals. He played with the Rangers for eight years before he was claimed by the Bruins in the waiver draft.

During those eight seasons, Hebenton averaged 22 goals and 24 assists per year. During the 1958–59 season, skating on a line with Red Sullivan at center and Camille Henry at the other wing, he scored 33 goals and set up 29 more.

"Sure I had some hurts now and then," Hebenton said. "But when I got them bad enough to miss a game I was always lucky enough to have a break in the schedule—a few nights when I could rest up."

4 Actually, all of them.

Let's do this chronologically.

When he was 15 years old, a shy but muscular Gordie Howe, who grew up in tiny Saskatoon, Saskatchewan, was invited to a Rangers tryout camp in Winnipeg by a scout named Russ McCrory. It was his first trip away from home, according to reports, and the boy who was assigned as his roommate was injured. Howe wasn't exactly accepted by the veterans, who kidded him daily. He confessed that he was "homesick and terribly lonely," wouldn't join the group for meals, and his family sent his train fare home in about a week.

The following year, 1944, Detroit Red Wings scout Fred Pinckney invited Howe to camp in nearby Winsdor, Ontario, with other teenagers from Saskatchewan to make him more comfortable. Howe impressed scouts with his strength and ability to shoot with either hand. He signed a $2,700 deal to play with the team's Junior A team and was promised a Red Wings jacket.

Two years later, in 1946, he was in the NHL and scored in his first game. The rest is history.

* * *

Joe Sakic, the 28-year-old captain of the Colorado Avalanche, had just led his squad to the Stanley Cup, and in August 1997 was a restricted free agent. Mark Messier had left the Rangers for free agency and general manager Neil Smith needed a replacement, so he took a bold shot at Sakic.

Smith signed Sakic to an offer sheet worth $21 million over three seasons, thinking that the financially troubled Avalanche couldn't match. He had sweetened the offer with a $15 million signing bonus on top of a $2 million annual salary.

"I know I'll be playing here in a place I love, or I'll be going to the great city of New York," Sakic said.

The choice for the Avalanche was this: accept the Rangers' next five first-round draft picks or pony up. They had a week to equal the offer and found it with some money from media companies.

Through some financial maneuvering involving Ascent Entertainment, which owned the Avalanche, Nuggets, and the future Pepsi Center (which would replace McNichols Aren), plus a $15 million investment from Liberty Media, the Avs avoided losing Sakic. Cable television rightsholder Fox Sports Rocky Mountain also agreed to extend its contract to televise Avalanche and Nuggets games for seven years.

Hard feelings? Well, Ascent chairman Charlie Lyons sent MSG President Dave Checketts a framed photo from 1976. It was then-US Vice President Nelson Rockefeller giving the middle finger to a group of hecklers in upstate New York.

* * *

Ziggy Palffy, a high-scoring right wing for the Islanders, almost went to Manhattan before the 1999 draft. The 27-year-old Slovak and defenseman Rich Pilon were all set to go to the Rangers for a package: forwards Niklas Sundstrom and Todd

Harvey, a 1999 first-round pick, a minor leaguer, and $2.5 million. The Islanders wanted Marc Savard included, which became a sticking point.

But the exchange also was scuttled when a dispute arose about how many Islanders games were to be shown the next season on Fox Sports New York, which was operated by Cablevision, the owner of the Rangers at the time.

That stalled the deal, and when the league balked at having cash included, discussions broke off.

* * *

In 2009, according to Rangers team president Glen Sather, he had a handshake deal with one of the Tampa Bay Lightning's co-owners, Len Barrie, to acquire Stamkos during his rookie season with the club. The talks, Sather later told the *New York Post*, began in Prague where the Rangers had opened the season with the Lightning and continued through Thanksgiving in Tampa.

Barrie wanted several players from a list that reportedly included Ryan Callahan, Brandon Dubinsky, Michael Del Zotto, Evgeny Grachev, and Dan Girardi.

Sather, who said he was assured by Barrie that he had the authority to make the swap, shook hands.

The next day, as the story goes, Sather said he learned that, in fact, Barrie needed approval from co-owner Oren Koules, "who shot it down," Sather said.

Close, but no cigar.

5 Mike Rupp.

Rupp, a 6-foot-5 grinder and former Devil in his first year in New York, suffered a knee injury in training camp and had played sparingly.

But late in the second period at Citizens Bank Park in Philadelphia on January 2, 2012, the Rangers were trailing 2-0 when Rupp's wrister went past Sergei Bobrovsky's glove and the Lakewood, Ohio, native saluted the benches, a gesture that appeared to mock All-World winger Jaromir Jagr, then playing for the Flyers, who had been saluting after scores.

Early in the third, Rupp flipped a softer shot from a bad angle to tie the game. Brad Richards scored the winner at 14:39, but the 3-2 game ended with some thrills and pot shots.

Asked about the taunt afterward, Rupp feigned innocence. "No, I, uh. . . . I don't know what you're talking about," he said. "I don't know what you're talking about." He then added, "I was just happy to get a goal, and I'll leave it at that."

In eight seasons, Rupp, then 32, had scored just 59 goals, although his second-period tip turned out to be the Stanley Cup clincher for the Devils over the Anaheim Mighty Ducks in 2003.

Jagr took the high road, but couldn't resist a parting jab. "I was hoping someone scored and we'd salute him back, but it just didn't happen. It's fine with me, it's not my signature," he said. "I do it because I'm celebrating a goal . . . He doesn't score many goals. Maybe that's the way he celebrates."

With 19.6 seconds left in regulation, the officials ruled that Ryan McDonagh had covered the puck with his glove in the crease and awarded a penalty shot to Danny Briere. Lundqvist made the save to clinch the 3-2 victory, but outspoken coach John Tortorella went out swinging, alleging collusion.

"Well I'm not sure if NBC got together with the refs, or what, to turn this into an overtime game," he said. "It started with the non-call on Gabby [Marian Gaborik], Gabby's walking in and he gets pitchforked in the stomach and then everything starts going against us. They are two good referees and I thought the game was reffed horribly. So I'm not sure what happened there, maybe they wanted to get it to an overtime. I'm not sure if they have meetings about that or what. But we stood in there. Again, they are good guys, but I just thought tonight, in that third period, it was disgusting."

Tortorella, who later apologized to the refs in person, added publicly: "It was wrong with my sarcasm and frustration, and I apologize to everyone involved. I want to make sure that's straight. That was not my intent and I certainly handled it the wrong way." Nonetheless, he was fined $30,000 by the NHL for his comments.

6 The Rangers have skated in four outdoor games, winning three.

They won the Winter Classic against the Flyers in Philadelphia on January 2, 2012, as well as two games in the Stadium Series against the Devils and Islanders at Yankee Stadium in late January 2014. The loss was the outdoor game that some people forget: A pre-season match against the Los Angeles Kings in the parking lot of Caesar's Palace in Las Vegas on September 27, 1991.

As more than 13,000 watched on a hot, sticky day that included a storm of grasshoppers, the Kings won 5-2.

The idea was to expose Wayne Gretzky to the masses, and Rich Rose, the sports director of Caesar's, pitched the idea to Roy Mlakar, the Kings' executive vice president of business operations, and Rangers general manager Neil Smith, who were friends.

The event itself was more newsworthy than the score. Construction began in the lot—which no longer exists—but where championship fights were held, with boxers such as Muhammad Ali. The rink was 192 feet, not 200, even though some stands were moved.

After the installed ice was ready—at a cost of $135,000—a tarp was laid down because the sun was out, bringing the temperature to the mid-90s. When the tarp warmed, the ice beneath began to melt.

But as the evening came, the temperature dropped into the 80s.

"I remember coming out and seeing [the rink] as a puddle, then actually having ice [after the Zamboni did some rounds]," Rangers goalie John Vanbiesbrouck told nhl.com.

Tony Amonte and Doug Weight scored in the first period, but Tony Granato, Brian Benning, and Sylvain Couturier countered to take a 3-2 lead after two. Jari Kurri and Gretzky scored in the third.

When the wave of bugs came, they dive-bombed into the ice and were caught in the slush. Ranger Tie Domi claimed he would've had a breakaway, but tripped because one of the locust-sized insects was caught in his skate.

"There was a little concern in that last six or seven minutes," Gretzky told nhl.com. "We didn't want to step wrong, pull a groin, break a leg or something like that, so we basically made a self-commitment in that last six minutes that nobody was going to go near anybody, nobody was going to hit anybody. Hey listen, we knew the conditions weren't perfect, so the players on both sides were really honest. Nobody wanted to hurt anybody, but they played hard. It just turned out to be a wonderful night, a nice game for everyone. And I think it went a long way to help promote our game in the Southwest."

For the Rangers, the first Stadium Series game against the Devils was delayed by an hour due to sun glare, and Dom Moore and other teammates tossed baseballs to warm up in the chill of the mid-20s. The Devils led 3-2 after the first period on two goals from Bobby Holik and one from Travis Zajac; Moore and Marc Staal scored for the Rangers. Mats Zuccarello, who was named the first star, scored the tying and go-ahead goals in the second. Devils goalie Martin Brodeur was pulled after the second period and Derek Stepan scored on a penalty shot against Cory Schneider in the third for the 7-3 final. Henrik Lundqvist made 19 saves.

Three days later, the Rangers beat the Islanders 2-1. Brock Nelson scored in the first period for the Islanders, but Benoit Pouliot tied it in the second and Daniel Carcillo won the game in the third. Lundqvist made 30 saves and raised his outdoor record to 3-0.

There are plans for a fifth outdoor game that includes the Rangers, another Winter Classic, on January 1, 2018, at Citi Field in New York, against the Buffalo Sabres.

7 Coach John Tortorella.

In the sixth game of the season—all on the road, as the Garden was undergoing a $1 billion facelift—the Rangers were blanked 2-0 by the Oilers in Edmonton on October 22, and Torts, steaming, was beside himself.

"This is gonna be really quick. I am not taking any questions. We sucked from head to toe and we need to move by it. So I'm not going to dissect with you guys. I know you have to do your job, but I'm not answering any questions. OK?"

He then walked off.

Tortorella, who could be curt, impatient, and have a tendency to belittle the media, has since taken a more restrained approach, at least publicly. But these remarks were among his more memorable during his tenure on Broadway.

Coaches speak daily during the season, not only to the press, but to players. Each handles the pressure differently.

Fred Shero, who led the Philadelphia Flyers to Stanley Cups in 1974 and 1975, had a much better way with language—and philosophy—than Tortorella. He also coached the Rangers for two seasons from June 1978 to November 1980. Called "The Fog" because of his cerebral thinking and also because he often seemed lost in thought, Shero motivated players in his own style, dishing out wisdom like assists.

Three of the more memorable:

"Success is not the result of spontaneous combustion. You must first set yourself on fire."

"Fame is a vapor, popularity an accident. Riches take wings. Only one thing endures, and that is character."

"Commitment is like ham and eggs. The chicken makes a contribution, the pig makes a commitment."

Jean Guy Talbot lasted a year less than Shero behind the bench, from August 1977 to June 1978. Talbot, a native of Quebec who played defense for the Canadiens for a dozen seasons starting in 1955 and spoke with a heavy accent, was fond of wearing a warm-up outfit rather than a business suit behind the bench.

Dave Maloney recalled players chuckling one night before a game in Toronto when Ron Low was the opposing goaltender. "Jean-Guy could not quite get it out whether we should 'shoot high on dat guy Low or low on dat guy High.'"

Talbot wasn't exactly deft with math either.

Unhappy with the offense, he once told the team that each of the 17 players should have two shots on goal. "Dat way we have 37."

8 Unfortunately, Ron Stewart, a defensive forward who had won three Stanley Cup championships in 13 seasons with the Toronto Maple Leafs, was engaged in a deadly fracas with Sawchuk.

The incident occurred after the 1969–1970 season, the only one that long-time Detroit Red Wing and four-time Vezina Award–winning goaltender Terry Sawchuk would play for the Rangers.

It didn't take place on the ice. They were teammates who shared a house in Atlantic Beach on Long Island, where, in the words of Nassau County district attorney William Cahn, the "tragic, senseless, bizarre" incident occurred on April 29, 1970.

An argument started at a nearby bar and finished with the pair grappling on the lawn of the house, where Sawchuk, then 40, fell and injured his gallbladder and liver. He underwent surgery three times, but died on May 31 of a blood clot at a hospital in Manhattan. A Nassau County grand jury found the death to be accidental, and Stewart was absolved of any blame. Sawchuk told police that he was the aggressor and responsible for the incident.

Emile Francis, the Rangers general manager and coach, had signed Sawchuk to back up Ed Giacomin and he had played eight games, going 3-1-2. Francis knew Stewart felt like an outcast and signed him for the following season.

Stewart later played for the Vancouver Canucks, the Rangers again, and the Islanders before retiring in 1973. Francis hired Stewart to succeed him as coach for the 1975–76 season. Stewart had a 15-20-4 record when John Ferguson replaced

Francis as general manager in January 1976 and then took over the coaching as well. Stewart then coached the Los Angeles Kings in 1977–78.

9 In the postseason, the Rangers have faced the Montreal Canadiens the most, 73 games, as of the end of the 2016–17 postseason. The Rangers won 9 of 16 series, with a record of 33-38-2. The Washington Capitals are a close second, with 55 games and a 27-28 record. The Blueshirts have played them five times since 2009 and won the last four series.

In the regular season, the Rangers have faced the Boston Bruins more than any other team: 643 times though the 2016–17 season. They have beaten them the most (255 times). The Rangers have lost the most times to the Canadiens, 330 out of 623 games.

10 Mats Zuccarello, the diminutive Norwegian winger, is the Rangers' all-time leader in shootout goals (19) and shootout attempts (38) as of April 2017. And he is in no danger of being caught soon.

When you hear "Zooooooooook" from fans in arenas, not only in the Garden, but on the road, where Norway team sweaters and signs abound, it's about No. 36.

Although he stands just 5-foot-7 and weighs less than 180 pounds, it's no surprise that Zuccarello, who teammates say has the best sense of where they are on the ice to receive passes, has succeeded in the NHL. Check the resume. In 2010, when he played for Modo Hockey, he won the Guldhjälmen (Golden Helmet), which is awarded annually to the most valuable player—according to other players—in the Swedish Hockey League.

Soon after, he was signed as a free agent and his touch and fearless style along the boards stood out on the smaller North American ice.

Zuccarello's career almost ended early in the 2015 Stanley Cup playoffs, when he was struck in the head by Ryan McDonagh's shot and he was hospitalized with a concussion and a brain bruise that affected his speech. He slowly recovered, but didn't return until the following season.

In an amazing comeback, Zuccarello scored a career-high 26 goals and posted 35 assists. That rebound on the ice prompted fans to reward him with the Steven McDonald Extra Effort Award for the second time and he also was selected as a finalist for the Bill Masterton Memorial Trophy.

Shootout goals don't count in the scoring total, but nonetheless, Zuccarello registered his 112th career NHL point and became the all-time leader in points by a Norwegian-born player on December 29, 2014. He passed Espen Knutsen.

NYR shootout goals (top 5)

1. Zuccarello 19
2. Michael Nylander 10
3. Brendan Shanahan 8
4. Derek Stepan 7
5. Erik Christensen 7

NYR shootout attempts (top 5)

1. Zuccarello 37
2. Michael Nylander 24
3. Brendan Shanahan 23
4. Jaromir Jagr 22
5. Derek Stepan 21

11 Centers Scott Gomez and Chris Drury, who inked lucrative multi-year, free-agent deals with the Rangers, each wanted to wear No. 23. Gomez, who wore 23 for both Stanley Cup teams in 2000 and 2002, offered it to Drury, who, at 30, was three years older.

Drury then suggested a coin flip. Rangers general manager Glen Sather tossed it and Drury won. Gomez ended up with No. 19.

The flip was an inexpensive way to decide. "I heard a rumor Paul Kariya once gave somebody two tickets to Hawaii for No. 9," veteran defenseman John Michael Liles told the *Toronto Star*. "I've heard about guys giving up a Rolex for a number, too. It was something that occurred more often than not."

As it turned out in this Rangers numbers game, there was a baseball connection for both players.

Drury, who was a pitcher on the Trumbull, Connecticut, team that won the Little League World Series in 1989, had worn No. 23 with his previous club, the Buffalo Sabres, in honor of Yankees first baseman Don Mattingly.

Gomez, who had been wearing 23 for the Devils, said he grew up wearing No. 11 and No. 19.

Carlos Gomez, Scott's father, was Mexican and a San Diego sports fan. Gomez admired No. 19 Hall of Famer Tony Gwynn, and in hockey, No. 19s Steve Yzerman and Joe Sakic.

"I don't think it would be that smart to [try to] get 11," Gomez said, referring to Mark Messier's digits. Blair Betts agreed to relinquish his No. 19 to Gomez, who donated $10,000 to a charity that Betts designated.

That was a drop in the bucket for Gomez. The Rangers needed centers to play with wingers Brendan Shanahan and Jaromir Jagr, so between the two players, were shelling out

Scott Gomez celebrates with Chris Drury (No. 23) and Marc Staal after scoring a shorthanded goal against the Pittsburgh Penguins on January 5, 2009, in the Garden. Gomez, who along with Drury signed free agent deals with the Rangers, had lost a coin flip to retain the number and switched to 19. (AP Photo/Julie Jacobson)

$86.75 million. Gomez had inked a seven-year deal worth $51.5 million; Drury's five-year contract was worth $35.25 million.

Drury had stuck a dagger in the Rangers just a few months earlier. In the second round of the playoffs against the Sabres, the Blueshirts had rebounded from a 2-0 deficit to tie the best-of-seven series. In Game 5, Drury scored the tying goal with 7.7 seconds left in regulation. The Sabres won the match in overtime and ended the series in Game 6.

Gomez played exactly two years wearing 19 in New York. He was traded to Montreal in July 2009 in a swap that brought prospect Ryan McDonagh to New York, a trade that still stings the Canadiens front office and their fans. Drury lasted four seasons. His knees were damaged, and he was bought out. Drury retired, but returned to the Rangers and was named assistant general manager in September 2016.

Both 19 and 23 are fairly common numbers. Some players want distinctive digits.

In 1977, Rangers goalie John Davidson struggled and switched from 30 to 00, thinking shutouts. No such luck. He had one that season and went 14-13-4. He backtracked to 30 for the 1978–79 season, and played far better as the Blueshirts advanced to the Stanley Cup Final.

The last goalie to wear 00 was Sabres backup goaltender Martin Biron, who would later become a Ranger. But he was forced to switch in 1998 when the NHL began requiring players to wear numbers from 1 to 98.

As far as many can tell, zero has been worn (briefly) by only one player: Hartford Whalers defenseman Neil Sheehy in 1988. When his family emigrated from Ireland, their name was O'Sheehy. He figured it was the best way to get the "O" on his back.

12 Jack Stoddard, Bob Brooke, Sergei Nemchinov, Valeri Kamensky, Richard Scott, Nikolai Zherdev, Dan Carcillo, Kevin Hayes.

In 1951, Stoddard, a right wing from Stoney Creek, Ontario, was acquired in a trade with the Providence Reds for Jean-Paul Denis, Pat Egan, and Zellio Toppazzini. He played 80 games from 1951 to 1953, scored 16 goals, and added 15 assists. At the time, he was the NHL's tallest player at 6-foot-3 and was the first Ranger to wear 13.

Brooke, an Acton, Massachussetts, native, became the first former Yale player to skate in the NHL when he debuted on March 9, 1984. The next day, Brooke, who played center and right wing, scored his first goal in Edmonton on a long slap shot that beat Grant Fuhr. He was the only Ranger to have a hat trick in the 1985–86 season, on November 20, 1985. His most memorable moment wearing the jersey came in Game 4 of the Patrick Division Finals on April 23, when he scored the tying goal with 2:35 left in regulation and the winner at 2:40 of overtime to beat the Capitals 6-5. That tied the series at two and the Rangers won the next two.

Nemchinov, a Moscow native chosen in the second round of the 1990 draft, was part of the first wave of European players who were not as affected by the superstition surrounding No. 13. As a rookie in 1992, he scored 30 goals to help the Rangers capture the Presidents' Trophy for the most points that season. In 1994, he scored 22 goals and 27 assists. He was traded to Vancouver during the 1996–97 season and is one of a handful of players to play for all three New York metropolitan-area teams, the Rangers, Devils, and Islanders.

Kamensky, a superb passer and effortless skater with a wicked slap shot, came to Broadway late in his career, at age 33, after winning the Cup with the Colorado Avalanche in 1996. In that season, he put up his most impressive numbers—38 goals and 47 assists—and was one of the top left wings in the

NHL. He spent two seasons with the Blueshirts, from 1999 to 2001, with 27 goals and 39 assists. Zherdev played just one season, 2008–09, and scored 23 goals.

Scott was a brawler who once collected 28 major penalties in the AHL and had no points in 10 games in 2001–02.

Carcillo, a rabble-rouser, played just 39 games for the Rangers—eight of them in the playoffs in 2013–14.

Hayes, who came from Boston College to the Rangers, played in his third season in 2016–17.

Valery Kamensky, one of the few Rangers to wear No. 13, searches for a rebound after Kings goalkeeper Stephane Fiset blocked his shot on Dec. 14, 2000, in Los Angeles. Kamensky played in New York from 1999 to 2001, and collected 27 goals and 39 assists. (AP Photo/Kevork Djansezian)

The most famous 13s in the NHL? Toronto's Mats Sundin and Detroit's Pavel Datsyuk.

13 Joe "Red Light" Miller, a former goalie who played for the New York Americans, the team that had shared Madison Square Garden with the Blueshirts that season, stepped up bigtime in the championship round.

Miller, 27, and the Americans did not qualify for the playoffs that season, so he went home to Morrisburg, Ontario, to relax.

Back in New York, the Rangers and Montreal Maroons were tied after two games of the best-of-five series. The big story was that in the second game, Rangers goalie Lorne Chabot was injured and 43-year-old general manager Lester Patrick took over and the Blueshirts won 2-1 in overtime. Chabot was ruled out for the rest of the series however, and there was no way Patrick, at his age, would return.

Without backup goalies, teams were allowed to borrow available short-term replacements. So Patrick asked Maroons coach Eddie Gerard if he could use veteran George Hainsworth, who had won the Vezina Trophy the previous two seasons, or Charlie Gardiner, who played for the Chicago Blackhawks, and were at the Montreal forum watching the series. Gerard refused.

After meetings with the league, Gerard allowed Miller, who was 8-16-4 with a 2.68 goals-against-average (high for the low-scoring NHL at the time) to be signed by the Rangers for the three games.

It initially looked like a smart move by Gerard. The Maroons won Game 3, 2-0, and apparently were planning a victory banquet after Game 4, Boucher once recalled.

But Boucher and Miller ruined the plans. Miller didn't allow a goal, and Boucher scored, tying the series and setting up a deciding game at the Forum on April 14, 1928.

Miller blanked the Maroons until there were five minutes left in regulation, when Bill Phillips scored, cutting the Rangers lead to 2-1, and held on for the unlikely victory.

The understudy-turned-hero didn't get another chance, however. Chabot was traded to Toronto, and Patrick acquired John Ross Roach. The Americans traded Miller to the Pittsburgh Pirates for Roy "Shrimp" Worters, who, at 5-foot-3, was only two inches shorter than Red Light.

Miller finished his career a year later with the Philadelphia Quakers. But he will be remembered for three games in a Rangers jersey.

14 Stan Brown was shipped to Detroit for Harry Meeking and Archie Briden on October 10, 1927. Neither ever played for the Blueshirts.

A star junior player in the Toronto area, Brown attended the University of Toronto and played amateur hockey until the 1926–27 season, when he joined the Detroit Greyhounds of the American Hockey Association. When the Greyhounds folded, Brown signed on with Lester Patrick's first Rangers team at midseason and played in the team's first playoff series against Boston in 1927.

Meeking's first pro season was with the Toronto Arenas team that won the Stanley Cup in the National Hockey League's inaugural season (1917–18) and recorded a playoff hat trick, a Stanley Cup first by a National Hockey League player.

The best cash deal was with the Montreal Maroons for Dave Kerr, on December 14, 1934, the goalie who won the team's Stanley Cup in 1940.

Of the hundreds of transactions—and thousands of opinions on those deals—there seems to be a consensus on the worst, at least when it comes to relatively big-name players.

It was an exchange of right wings in May 1976.

General manager John Ferguson was persuaded by Phil Esposito, who wanted former Bruins linemate Ken Hodge, and sent 22-year-old Rick Middleton to Boston for Hodge.

Middleton, who had scored 22 and 24 goals in his first two years as a Blueshirt, exploded out of the gates in Beantown, scoring at least 40 goals and 90 points in each of the next five seasons. In 12 seasons there, he collected 402 goals and almost 900 points.

Hodge, then 32, was an outright bust. He scored 23 goals in a little more than a season, before being sent down to New Haven, the team's AHL affiliate, and retired soon thereafter.

15 No, not Ulf Nilsson, perhaps the best-known Ulf, but Ulf Sterner was the first Swede to play—albeit briefly—for the Rangers.

Ulf Ivar Erik "Uffe" Sterner was a star center in Sweden, having played in nine IIHF World Championships and in the 1960 Olympics, where NHL teams took notice. The Rangers invited Sterner to training camp in 1963, and agreed to a five-game tryout, but Sterner declined, opting to remain an amateur to qualify for the 1964 Winter Olympics, where Sweden would win a silver medal.

In the next training camp, Sterner needed to adjust to the North American game, where checking was allowed in all zones; the IIHF rules prohibited hitting in the offensive zone. So Sterner went first to St. Paul of the Central League and then to the Baltimore Clippers, where he went 18-26-44 before he was called up and joined the Rangers at age 23 to debut against the Boston Bruins on January 27, 1965. He played just four games and didn't record a point, mostly because of his reluctance to engage in the more physical style, and was assigned to the AHL. He eventually returned to Sweden.

Nilsson starred, but there was a villain in his career arc.

On February 23, 1979, Isles defenseman Denis Potvin lined up Nilsson for a hip check, and the hit broke the Swede's ankle, sidelining him for the rest of the season.

Potvin wasn't penalized, and to this day, he is serenaded at least once at home games after the crowd is cued by a whistle and chants: "Pot-vin sucks!"

Anders Hedberg was the other notable Swede of that era, long before Henrik Lundqvist.

Playing on a line with the WHA's Winnipeg Jets with Nilsson and Bobby Hull, Hedberg led the circuit with 70 goals in 1976–77. The next summer Sonny Werblin enticed them to New York for $2.4 million, a huge sum at the time.

Hedberg dazzled with 33 goals and 78 points as the Rangers marched to the Stanley Cup Final.

Like Nilsson, he was slowed by injuries, losing most of the 1982–83 season to knee surgery. In each of his six full seasons with the Blueshirts, though, the right wing scored at least 20 goals and 50 points, and is the highest-scoring European in franchise history, with 172 goals and 225 assists, 17th on the all-time list.

16 The Chiefs: Defenseman Jim Neilson, part Cree Indian and part Dane, patrolled the Rangers blue line from 1962 to 1974, mostly with partner Rod Seiling. Robert Comas, a Brooklyn native, was an unofficial mascot who wore a Native American headdress and face paint and rallied fans in the stands starting in 1971.

Neilson is perhaps the most under-rated defenseman of the franchise. With 810 games as a Ranger, only three blue-liners played more: Harry Howell, Ron Greschner, and Brian Leetch.

At 6-foot-2, Neilson was a non-flamboyant, physical player who had offensive skills and was often deployed on left wing. In fact, he scored the first goal of his career as a forward against the Boston Bruins at Boston Garden in his rookie season. But his defensive game excelled. He was a top-shelf body checker and effective with the poke check, and was known as a gentleman off the ice.

During a game on February 13, 1970, against the Oakland Seals, he suffered a serious knee injury, and later wore a special brace designed by orthopedist Dr. James A. Nicholas. Only one other athlete had tried the brace before: Jets quarterback Joe Namath. He eventually changed to a more flexible one, but his skating was never the same. Although the Rangers amassed 100 or more points for the next three seasons, Neilson was left unprotected at the 1974 inter-league draft and after some dispute, became a California Golden Seal.

The Seals had agreed to take Neilson with the first overall pick and drop Walt McKechnie from their protected list, to be claimed by the Blueshirts as compensation, and would later trade him to the Bruins for Derek Sanderson. But Sabres general manager Punch Imlach tried to claim McKechnie, a move that was prohibited by the league because each team could only lose one player.

Comas, the non-playing "Chief," was a fixture at home games, stirring up the crowd with whoops and war dances, and he put the outfit into mothballs in 1995, a year after the Rangers won the Stanley Cup. Always interested in politics as well as sports, Comas ran as a Conservative Party candidate for State Senate in his district in 1998, but lost to the incumbent. After moving to Florida, he died at age 62.

17 John Ferguson, Sr., the former Montreal Canadiens legend who was more of an enforcer than a fashion consultant, tried to mess with the classic sweater during the 1976–77 season.

When Ferguson, who started his career as a bodyguard for young Canadiens such as Jean Beliveau and Boom-Boom Geoffrion and later ordered Bobby Clarke to injure Soviet star Valeri Kharlamov in the 1972 Summit Series against Team Canada, became the Rangers general manager, he wanted a new look.

So he dumped the style that had been the template since the 1920s: the new jersey was a darker shade of blue, with red and white striping, rounded numbers, and an oversized shield on the chest. It caused a stir immediately, but was worn for the 1977–78 season as well. Ferguson was fired in the offseason, the traditional look returned in the 1978–79 season, and coincidence or not, the Rangers went to the Stanley Cup Final.

Ferguson became general manager of the Winnipeg Jets of the World Hockey Association and, undaunted, ordered a similar re-design. The Jets won the AVCO Cup, but the league folded.

18 St. Louis Blues defenseman Steve Durbano.

On February 21, 1979, with about 12 minutes to play in a game that the Rangers would win 7-3, Durbano and Nick Fotiu started what turned into a bench-clearing melee.

In 1971, Durbano had actually been a first-round draft pick of the Rangers, but was traded to the Blues. He was an out-of-control player with a string of suspensions in every league he played in. Durbano appeared in just 220 NHL games and averaged just over five penalty minutes per game.

Fotiu, the popular Staten Island native who was the first Ranger raised in the city and, as a fan, had watched games from high above in the blue-collar seats, was a former amateur boxer.

The pair had bumped on the ice after a Blues goal, and Durbano swung his stick at Fotiu, who tried to respond in kind as players gathered in a scrum near the benches. The would-be combatants were separated after a few minutes, but Durbano broke free and charged across the ice for another run at Fotiu, and each landed a blow before they were wrestled apart.

As Durbano skated off alone toward the exit doors at one corner of the rink to the visiting locker room, the noise of the loud crowd in the background, he turned backward, bending over.

When Fotiu saw that, he went berserk, charging through the tunnel behind the benches, shoving officials, and heading for the corridor that connected the two dressing rooms to intercept Durbano. "There'd better be a cop between them," said radio color commentator Bill Chadwick.

Security personnel intervened and prevented an off-ice bout. Durbano, who had been suspended three times since 1974, was suspended for five games; Fotiu was fined $450. And before the next home game, a locked door was installed in the corridor between the rooms.

19 From 1954 to 1961, "Leaping Louie" Fontinato was the beat cop for the Rangers and one of toughest little guys in the league.

Fontinato wasn't big—a little jump off his skates to deliver a hard check or to dispute a penalty gave him the nickname—but his work ethic and heart went unchallenged. In six full seasons with the Blueshirts (418 games), he served 939 minutes in penalties and led the NHL in infractions in the 1955–56 and 1957–58 seasons.

His punch that bloodied Montreal icon Maurice Richard made headlines, but his long-running feud with Gordie Howe, the Red Wings scoring legend who had a mean streak, was

"Leaping Louie" Fontinato (5), the beat cop for the Rangers from 1954 to 1961, didn't stay on his feet often when he bodied opponents or complained to referees. He did here against forward Tod Sloan to protect maskless goalie Gump Worsely in a game against the Toronto Maple Leafs at the Garden on November 10, 1954. (AP Photo)

well-chronicled, with the most notable bout at Madison Square Garden on February 1, 1959.

In the first period, after Howe chopped the Rangers' Eddie Shack in the side of the head with his stick and as the refs were trying to settle down the scrum, like a bullet, Fontinato flew in from mid-ice and sucker-punched Howe with three lefts. Bad move.

Howe landed five blows that sent Fontinato first to the ice and then to the emergency room with a broken cheekbone and nose, a split lip, and a cut over the eye. A large photo of the battered Blueshirt was featured in *Life Magazine*.

In 1963, his career ended with a check into the boards from Vic Hadfield. Fontinato, who was playing for the Canadiens, broke his neck. His arms and legs were paralyzed for weeks, and though he eventually recovered, Fontinato retired.

20 Almost 70 years ago, the Rangers were the first NHL team to sign a black player, Art Dorrington, from Truro, Nova Scotia, who signed a contract in 1950.

On his first trip to the US, Dorrington, then 20, was with a Connecticut minor-league team that practiced at the Garden and a scout offered him a contract to play for the team's affiliate, the New York Rovers, who were on a road trip.

"I was in a hotel in New York City by myself for four days and I felt homesick," Dorrington said years later. "I got impatient, so I told the Rangers that I needed to play some hockey. They arranged for me to go to Atlantic City for a weekend tryout with a team they had a working agreement with."

No black player had skated for a pro team until the 5-foot-8 Dorrington spent eight years with the Atlantic City Sea Gulls of the Eastern Hockey League, scoring 151 goals and

152 assists for 303 points in 336 regular season games. In 1951, the Gulls won the EHL championship and Dorrington had 18 goals and 16 assists. During the summer, he played center field for teams in the Boston Braves organization in upstate New York.

Dorrington played for six different Eastern League teams. With the Johnstown Jets in 1952–53, he scored 25 goals and 30 the next season. He continued to fill the net at his next stop, the Washington Lions, when he scored 33, and 33 again for the Philadelphia Ramblers in 1955–56.

Racism had deep roots in some cities. "I went to places like Washington, Charlotte, Greensboro and the rest of the team would go to a hotel or restaurant, and I wouldn't be allowed to go in. I had to put up with the same kind of racism that Jackie Robinson put up with in baseball," he told writers back in Atlantic City, where he settled when his career was over.

Dorrington, who had become a US citizen, was drafted and returned to the Ramblers in 1958. While playing a game in Utica, he was lugging the pucks and was tripped and broke his left leg. He had played just 11 games.

After four operations, he retired in 1961. "I lost my speed," he recalled. "I didn't consider [the injury] a racial thing. I don't. I just beat a guy on a play and he stuck his leg out. Most of the Eastern League players were Canadians. We had more in common than not."

21 Don Maloney notched the fastest hat trick—a trio of goals against Washington. Maloney scored at 16:41, 18:37, and 19:11 (2:30 total) of the second period on February 21, 1981, at the Garden against Mike Palmateer. Maloney, a terrific left wing, would have three other hat tricks in his Rangers career.

One of them had come just a few weeks before, on February 4, against the Islanders' Billy Smith.

His best season came in 1982–83, when he scored 29 goals and 69 points in 78 games.

Maloney actually finished his playing career with the Islanders and became the team's general manager, then assistant general manager for the Rangers, and later, general manager of the Phoenix Coyotes.

The first hat trick at the original MSG?

Veteran left wing Don Maloney (right) joins rookie Brian Leetch during the defenseman's first practice as a Ranger on Feb. 28, 1988. Maloney had four hat tricks in his career, including the fastest in Rangers history (in two minutes and 30 seconds) on Feb. 21, 1981, against Washington at the Garden. (AP Photo/Ray Stubblebine)

That came from Murray Murdoch, who swept two goals in a 10-second span past Chicago goalkeeper Hugh Lehman and recorded the game-winning goal with 1:10 remaining in regulation as the Rangers defeated the Black Hawks, 5-4 on January 16, 1927.

Murdoch played in 11 consecutive seasons, never missing a single game. In total, he played in 508 straight regular-season games, as well as 55 Stanley Cup playoff matches.

After he reached 400 games, the Rangers honored him at the Garden. Yankees first baseman Lou Gehrig, baseball's most famous iron man, who played an astounding 2,130 major-league games in a row, presented Murdoch with a plaque commemorating the occasion.

The Rangers all-time leader in hat tricks is Bill Cook, with 11. He scored all 11 between November 1926 and March 1933. His first trick was the first in franchise history, against John Ross Roach on November 20, 1926, in a 5-1 roasting of Toronto.

Think 11 is a lot? Wayne Gretzky, who leads the NHL in hat tricks, had 50. That's not a typo.

No hats or knit caps floated down from the stands and drifted to the ice in the days of Murray Murdoch and you'd have to go back more than a century for the origin of the term.

The first recorded usage of "hat trick" came after a cricket match in 1858 when English bowler Heathfield Harman "HH" Stephenson took three consecutive wickets for the All-England Eleven against the twenty-two of Hallam, South Yorskshire, at Hyde Park Grounds, Sheffield. Afterward, a collection was taken (as was customary for outstanding play) and Stephenson was presented with a cap or hat bought with the proceeds.

Although both a haberdashery in Guelph, Ontario, says they too offered hats to players who scored three goals, the Hockey Hall of Fame calls this the official version.

Alex Kaleta, a Chicago Blackhawks winger, stopped into Sammy Taft's Toronto haberdashery in January 1946 before a game with the Maple Leafs. Kaleta adored a gray fedora with a gray silk band.

Having just returned from serving in the Canadian military during World War II, Kaleta couldn't afford the chapeau. So Taft proposed that if Kaleta scored three goals against the Leafs that night, January 26, 1946, he could have the hat for free.

Well, Kaleta did him one better: he scored four times (although the Blackhawks lost 6-5). Taft then continued with the "trick" of giving a free hat to any player who scored three goals in a game at Maple Leaf Gardens, and a hockey phrase was born.

In the 1950s, the Guelph Biltmore Mad Hatters of the Ontario Hockey Association (a Rangers farm team) were sponsored by Biltmore Hats. According to some, they would give a brand-new fedora to any Mad Hatters player who scored three goals in a game.

During the 1970s, fans began tossing their own headwear on the ice of a three-goal display, and the league eventually amended its rule book to read that "articles thrown onto the ice following a special occasion (i.e. hat trick) will not result in a bench minor penalty being assessed" to the home team for delay of the game.

Hats that are collected by ice crews are offered to the player—some keep one or two as a memento—and the rest are donated to charities or local hospitals or displayed in arenas.

Some fans take it a little too far. At NHL and college games and sometimes overseas, everything from octopi to catfish to plastic rats to waffles to sex toys to stuffed animals are flung on the ice, sometimes after just one goal!

Before we return to the Rangers tricksters, it's impossible to write about hat tricks without including the tale of Bill "Wee Willie" Mosienko.

In March 1952, Mosienko, a Ukrainian forward who had played nine years for the Blackhawks, was concluding his highest-scoring season, and met an old friend in Toronto for drinks and dinner.

"We were thumbing through the NHL record book," Mosienko later recalled, "and I remarked how nice it would be to have my name in there with some of the hockey greats. But I just figured it would never happen—and then it did, 48 hours later."

On Saturday, Mosienko scored two goals, including the winner, in a 3-2 edging of the Leafs, and the team left for the final game of the season, Sunday, March 23, at, where else, Madison Square Garden.

Both clubs were out of playoff contention, and fewer than 5,000 paying customers were gathered in the lower bowl. Lorne Anderson, a 20-year-old third-string goalie, was in net because the Rangers starting tandem of Emile Francis and Chuck Rayner were not in the lineup.

Nonetheless, the Blueshirts led 6-2 in the third period, when Mosienko caught fire—and caught Anderson napping.

He took Gus Bodnar's pass and beat Anderson at 6:09. Bodnar won the next faceoff and saw Mosienko racing for the crease alone, having split the defense. He put the puck past Anderson at 6:20! Seconds later, Bodnar's faceoff win went to forward George Gee, who passed to Mosienko, who finished the play at 6:30 for three goals in 21 seconds, an NHL record that still stands.

About 45 seconds later, as Mosienko told *Hockey Digest*, he had the puck again, faked Anderson, and wristed a shot that missed the far post by inches.

When Mosienko skated to the bench, coach Ebbie Good-fellow reportedly shouted: "Hey Mosie, what the heck happened? You slowing down?"

Chicago won 7-6. For Anderson, it was the third and final game of his career.

The closest anyone has come to eclipsing Mosienko's feat was on November 5, 1954. Canadiens legend Jean Beliveau scored three times in 44 seconds against Detroit's Terry Sawchuk while Montreal was on a 5-on-3 power play. At that time, a penalized player served the entire two minutes of a minor penalty.

The following summer, the NHL changed the rule: minor penalties would now end after a goal.

The vote was 5 to 1; Montreal was the only team to vote against it.

Including the 2016–17 season, Rangers players have scored 248 hat tricks.

Here's the rest of the top 10:

Rod Gilbert 7

Frank Boucher 6

Mark Messier 6

Jean Ratelle 6

Petr Nedved 6 (The Czech winger had four between 1999 and 2001.)

Adam Graves 5

Andy Bathgate 5

Ron Duguay 5

Marian Gaborik 5

Besides Don Maloney, whose defense-minded brother Dave had one against Minnesota's Gilles Meloche at the Garden on March 9, 1980, 10 other players had four hat tricks in their Rangers career.

They are: Bun Cook, Cecil Dillon, Darren Turcotte, Dave Balon, Dean Prentice, Don Raleigh, Grant Warwick, Pierre Larouche, Tomas Sandstrom, and Wally Hergesheimer.

Many players would sell their souls to have one hat trick a year. But in the 1986–87 season, Sandstrom established a franchise record for three-or-more-goal nights in a single campaign.

On March, 4, 1987, Sandstrom registered his fourth hat trick of the season. He collected three goals as the Rangers defeated the Islanders, 7-5, at home.

Sandstrom, the best player ever to wear No. 28 for the Blueshirts, excelled on the international level. In 1987 at the World Championships in Vienna, his last-minute goal, on a pass from Hakan Loob, tied the game against the USSR, and the Swedish National Team moved on to beat Canada for the gold medal.

Three years prior, at age 20, he won the bronze medal at the Winter Olympics in Sarajevo and was on Sweden's second-place team at the Canada Cup in 1984 and third-place squad at the 1991 Canada Cup. After his time with the Rangers, starting in 1984, when he scored 380 points in 407 games, he won the Stanley Cup with the Red Wings in 1997.

Balon had four tricks in a very short span as well: February 10, 1970, against Pittsburgh's Al Smith; April 25, 1970, against Roger Crozier when he was with the Red Wings; December

22, 1970, against Crozier with Buffalo, and January 24, 1971, versus Minnesota's Gilles Gilbert.

Those three-goal games came in Balon's second stint with the Rangers. He had been traded to the Canadiens in a deal for goalie Jacques Plante, and the left wing won Stanley Cups with the Habs, first in 1965 and then in 1966, when he assisted on Henri Richard's Cup-clinching goal in overtime.

Balon was reclaimed in the first-ever expansion draft, and on the "Bulldog Line" with Walt Tkaczuk and Bill Fairbairn from 1968 to 1971, Balon led the Rangers in goals twice. Unfortunately, his career was cut short by multiple sclerosis, and he retired after the 1973–74 season with Vancouver.

Time out. If we had sponsors, there could be some commercials here.

Do you know who was the first Rangers defenseman to record a hat trick? Brad Park, when the Rangers defeated the Pittsburgh Penguins, 6-1, at the Garden on December 12, 1971.

Time in.

Since 2006, there have only been 24 hat tricks, including three in the 2016–17 season: Michael Grabner on October 30 in a 6-1 win; Matt Puempel, the first of his career, on December 29 in a 6-3 win in Arizona, and Chris Kreider on December 31, in a 6-2 win in Colorado. It was Kreider's second hat trick and came against Calvin Pickard.

Puempel and Kreider were the first Rangers to generate hat tricks in consecutive games on one road trip since March 22-24, 1978, when Ron Greschner scored three goals in a 6-1 win at St. Louis and Phil Esposito and Ron Duguay both scored three times in an 11-4 victory at Washington.

That's a rarity in itself: two tricks in one game.

Believe it or not, some players don't even recall their triples.

"I don't remember my last one," said Grabner, the Austrian-born winger with upper-torso tattoos that resemble those of a mixed martial arts fighter. The former Islander had signed a free-agent contract with the Rangers during the summer. "I think it was against Buffalo, don't know the year, but it's nice to get another one." Grabner was at least right about the team. It was February 13, 2011, against the Sabres, and he scored the winner in overtime.

Grabner's Rangers teammate, center Derek Stepan, had a hat trick to remember.

On October 9, 2010, Stepan scored three times in his NHL debut against Ryan Miller of the Sabres.

Stepan, the Minnesota native who played at the University of Wisconsin with Ryan McDonagh before the Rangers, was part of another hat-trick double.

He and Rick Nash turned tricks in consecutive home games: December 23, 2014 (Nash against Washington's Braden Holtby), and Stepan on December 27, 2014, against Cory Schneider, who allowed two of the three. The last one was an empty-netter.

Before Nash and Stepan's back-to-backers, the last time the Blueshirts had a hat trick in two straight games was back in 1994: Mike Gartner scored three against Pittsburgh on January 31, and Adam Graves matched that against the Islanders on February 2. The Puempel-Kreider tandem was the most recent of that ilk.

No discussion of Rangers hat tricks would be complete without Steve Vickers's feat.

Vickers made NHL history in 1972 when he became the first rookie, as well as the first Ranger, to record hat tricks in consecutive games. On November 12, he lit up Gary Edwards of the Los Angeles Kings; and on November 15 against Michel Belhumeur of the Philadelphia Flyers.

Undoubtedly, the most critical time to score a hat trick would be in the playoffs, right?

Fifteen times, Rangers have scored three goals in the Stanley Cup playoffs. The last such hat trick was from center Derick Brassard, who scored three on May 26, 2015, in Tampa in Game 6 of the Eastern Conference Semifinals.

By the way, there are two definitions of natural hat tricks. The first is a player scoring three goals in a single period. The second (and more common) is a player scoring three goals in a row, with no other player scoring in between.

The great Mark Messier did both in one of the most clutch performances in playoff history. So let's wrap up this hat trick seminar with that one.

It was Game 6 of the 1994 Eastern Conference Finals, May 25, and The Moose had basically guaranteed a win. Magically, it occurred.

With the Rangers trailing 2-1 entering the third period, center Alexei Kovalev, who had been switched to Messier's wing from his usual spot on the second line, slid a pass to No. 11, who backhanded a shot past Martin Brodeur's left pad to tie the game at 2:48.

The celebratory mood in the Meadowlands Arena changed. The teams shared chances for about 10 minutes, and at four a side, Kovalev's slap shot from the lower left circle bounced off Brodeur's chest and dropped to the ice. Messier, cutting through the slot, found the gift and made no mistake, swiping the puck in. Mess had two, and the Rangers had three, and the lead.

Now trailing by a goal, Brodeur was pulled, and with a Ranger in the penalty box, it was 6 on 4 with about two minutes remaining.

Messier intercepted a pass by John MacLean in the Rangers zone and lifted the puck toward the wide open cage from what appeared to be 500 feet away.

"For the empty net, Mark Messier," shouted broadcaster Gary Thorne. "Do you believe it? Do you believe it? He said, 'We will win Game 6'—he just picked up the hat trick!"

22 Twenty-two players scored four goals in a game for the Blueshirts. Rod Gilbert accomplished the feat three times, and Steve Vickers twice.

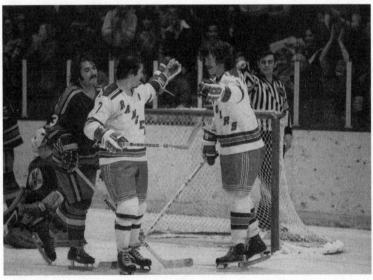

Steve Vickers (right) reacts to the first of his four goals on March 31, 1975, against the Kansas City Scouts at Madison Square Garden. Vickers would score a quartet in a game twice in his Rangers career, and Rod Gilbert, celebrating with Vickers, did it four times. (AP Photo/Ray Stubblebine)

The rest, and there are some names here that you wouldn't expect, did it once:

Bill Cook, Camille Henry, Jean Ratelle, Mark Messier, Phil Esposito, Marian Gaborik, Cecil Dillon, Dave Balon, Dean Prentice, Don Raleigh, Tomas Sandstrom, Anders Hedberg, Tony Granato, Greg Polis, Radek Dvorak, Ryan Callahan, Rick Middleton, Tony McKegney, Nick Mickoski, and Wally Hergesheimer.

Mickoski, called Broadway Nick, had one 20-goal season for the Rangers. In 1950–51, he scored four goals at Madison Square Garden on December 24, 1950, against Harry Lumley of Chicago.

The smallish Hergesheimer, a right wing who played in the early 1950s with parts of two fingers missing after an accident with an industrial punch-press, was known as the "Garbage Collector" for managing to find space in front of the net for loose pucks. He netted four against Chicago's Al Rollins on November 3, 1953.

Dillon was one of the few American-born players in the NHL at the time. He was born in Toledo, Ohio, but grew up in Ontario. A right wing who shot from the left side, Dillon played nine years with the Blueshirts, often on a line with Murray Murdoch and Butch Keeling, and was part of that trio when the Rangers won the Stanley Cup in 1933. Dillon was the undisputed scoring star of that squad, with eight goals and 10 points in eight games. His four-goal night came on January 28 in Ottawa, against Alec Connell in a 9-2 win. From 1936 through 1938 he led the Rangers in scoring three consecutive years. Only Frank Boucher, Bill Cook, Andy Bathgate, Phil Esposito, and Wayne Gretzky would match that.

McKegney played 912 games with seven different teams, but his four-goal game came in his only season with the Rangers. He was acquired from Minnesota with Curt Giles and a second-round draft pick for Bob Brooke and Minnesota's 4th round pick on November 13, 1986.

He would score 29 goals in 64 games that season, including the four in Vancouver on November 21, 1986. Three were against Wendel Young, and a fourth against Richard Brodeur in an 8-5 win. The following year, when he was sent to St. Louis, he scored 40, a career-high.

Quiet, unassuming Dean Prentice, a two-way player who had played with Andy Bathgate, Lou Fontinato, and Harry Howell in juniors, came to the Rangers and filled a role. He backchecked, killed penalties, and helped Bathgate and Larry Popein become the most successful line in the mid-50s to early 1960s. He played 10 seasons in New York, and his four-goal game came against Toronto goaltending legend Johnny Bower, at Madison Square Garden on November 19, 1958, in a 7-4 win.

Cammy Henry's four were against another goaltending icon, Terry Sawchuk, in Detroit, during a 5-2 victory on March 13, 1954. Henry, called "The Eel" for his ability to slip past checks and create plays, was an easy fellow to like.

He won the Calder Cup as top rookie in 1954, with 39 points in 66 games. He spent the next season between the Rangers and the Providence Reds, and two years later, led the AHL in goals with 50 goals, and added 41 assists in just 59 games. He also scored 10 goals in nine playoff games. That was enough to eventually give him another shot on Broadway.

In the 1957–58 season, he scored 32 goals and 24 assists in 70 and had just two penalty minutes, earning him the Lady

Byng Trophy. His best NHL season was in 1962–63. That was a point-a-game year: 37 goals and 23 assists in 60 games.

23 Two players scored nine seconds after the puck dropped: Ron Duguay on April 6, 1980, in Philadelphia and Jim Wiemer did it on March 27, 1985, in Buffalo.

The quickest goal at the start of a game at Madison Square Garden was scored in 2008 by a player with a reputation as a pest rather than a finisher: Sean Avery. He did it on February 16 against Ryan Miller in a 5-1 defeat of the Buffalo Sabres, with assists from Brandon Dubinsky and Jaromir Jagr at the 10-second mark. Avery also scored the team's final goal against Jocelyn Thibault at 7:47 of the second period.

Scoring rapidly—in bunches—by a player or players doesn't happen much these days. After two quick goals, coaches often call time-outs to break the momentum.

But sometimes, it snowballs.

It was like a lightning bolt that struck in the first period against the Colorado Rockies (not the current baseball team, of course) on January 14, 1980. Doug Sulliman, Eddie Johnstone, and Warren Miller scored in a 28-second span, the fastest trio of goals in Rangers history.

Sulliman was in good company when he was picked in the first round of the 1979 entry draft by the Rangers. Among his fellow first-rounders: soon-to-be-stars Ray Bourque, Michel Goulet, Brian Propp, and Mike Gartner. On that night, he scored one of his four goals of the season at 7:52. Sulliman would later post five 20-goal seasons for the Hartford Whalers and New Jersey Devils.

Johnstone followed five seconds later. The feisty right wing would have consecutive 30-goal seasons before being traded to Detroit with Ron Duguay and goalie Eddie Mio for Mike Blaisdell, Willie (Baby) Huber, and Mark Osborne in 1983.

Miller, a star at the University of Minnesota, nevertheless was picked in the 21st round, 241st overall in 1974, one of the lowest picks possible. He finished the trifecta at 8:20. To his credit, he played 500 games in the WHA and NHL, including 55 with the Rangers.

Oddly enough, the Rangers didn't win the game. It ended in a 6-6 tie.

About five years later, four Rangers took a shade longer to score four. It was February 15, 1985, again at Madison Square Garden and again in the first period. Do you sense a pattern?

The opponent this time was the Edmonton Oilers, and a quartet far more familiar to fans dealt the blows.

Former US Olympian Mark Pavelich found the net at 15:53, and Mike Rogers followed at 16:18. Ron Greschner hit the twine at 16:51 and Rogers zeroed in again at 17:31.

That was Rogers's last full season with the Rangers, and he scored 26 goals. The smallish, former WHA center played on lines with Gordie Howe and son Mark with the New England Whalers (later established in Hartford in 1979). There, he played with Pat Boutette and Blaine Stoughton on the "Stash-Dash-Bash" line (yes, the speedy Rogers was the "Dash"). He scored 105 points in each of his two seasons there. He arrived in New York in 1981, after a swap for Kris Kotsopoulos and the aforementioned Doug Sulliman. In his first campaign with the Rangers Rogers scored 103 points, including 38 goals.

By the way, the day the foursome struck for four, the home team won, 8-7.

Which brings us, dear fans, to this: the fastest five goals in your team's checkered history.

It was just a few seasons ago: April 19, 2013. Naturally, the way things change in the NHL nowadays, none of the players are still with the club.

This barrage took less than three minutes: 2:58 to be exact. And it stretched from the first to the second period, but not in New York (well, upstate New York, in Buffalo) in an 8-4 win.

The names and numbers: Carl Hagelin (18:42), Brad Richards (19:39), Ryane Clowe (19:56), Anton Stralman (1:13), and Richards again at 1:40. Four of the goals were against Ryan Miller; the fifth eluded replacement Jhonas Enroth. Richards would nail down the hat trick in the third period.

Hagelin later had a brief stop in Anaheim before winning a Cup in Pitttsburgh. Richards was bought out. Clowe had to retire because of injuries, and Anton Stralman fled to Tampa via free agency.

24 Pierre Larouche.

They called him "Lucky Pierre," a handsome young guy from Quebec, with quick hands made for scoring and a knack for finding the puck in the right spot to shoot.

In 1976, with the Penguins, Larouche became the youngest player to hit the 50-goal and 100-point plateau, with 53 goals and 11 points, and stayed there until that record was broken by Wayne Gretzky in 1980. He was the first player to score 50 goals in a season with two different teams: He scored 50 with Montreal in 1979–80. And then he fired in 48 for the Rangers in 1983–84.

But Larouche had another side: he could be moody, loved the nightlife a wee bit too much, and openly disdained playing defense. He once told teammates that he was paid $150,000 a year to score goals, and "if they want me to play defense, they can pay me another $150,000."

After a sensational junior career, he collected 31 goals and 37 assists in his rookie season in Pittsburgh at 19, and the city fell for him as much as they had for Steelers quarterback and bon vivant Terry Bradshaw.

But his production slipped, the veneer began to crack, the media started to turn, and with less than two months gone in the 1977–78 season and Larouche asking to be traded, the

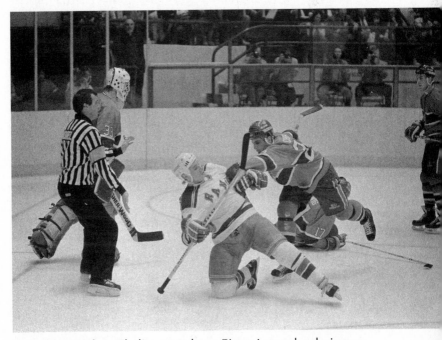

Defenseman Chris Chelios tugs down Pierre Larouche during a game on May 5, 1986, but few opponents could corral Larouche, a gifted offensive player with flair who netted 48 goals in 1983–84 and scored at almost a point-a-game pace in four seasons in New York. (AP Photo/Ray Stubblebine)

Penguins dealt him to the Canadiens, where he was on the 1978 and 1979 Stanley Cup championship teams, and then was shipped to the Hartford Whalers, and eventually, the Rangers.

"He was an arrogant bastard to play against, but when I got to know him, I thought he was a great guy," said Dave Maloney.

At age 28, Larouche netted 48 goals for the Rangers, and for four seasons scored at almost a point-a-game pace. In 253 games, he had 243 points. In 27 playoff games, he put up 26 points.

"Playing that year (1983–84) for Herb Brooks—he was pretty special. We had a real good team, but ran into the Islanders [in the divisional semifinals of the playoffs], played them five games and then lost in overtime," he once recalled. "They were a great team, but we should have beaten them that year. I still shake my head because we outplayed them, but we couldn't get over that hump and they went on to win the Cup. That [Ken] Morrow goal [in overtime of the deciding Game 5] . . . Glen Hanlon never saw it. I still think about it."

25 Ron Duguay, Phil Esposito, Dave Maloney, and Anders Hedberg skated in their white jerseys—and tight-fitting denims of course—and sang the jingle in the first of the campaigns for the jeans in 1979. Ron Greschner replaced Duguay in the 1980 version, in which their sports jackets magically changed into their jerseys after two young women admirers watching the ice dancers asked, "Who are those guys?"

The company went bankrupt six years later.

The clock has ticked off the last few seconds. The horn sounds. We're going to overtime.

Why? Like the NHL, we prefer winners and losers, not ties.

On June 23, 1983, the NHL introduced a regular-season overtime period of five minutes. If the period ended with no scoring, the game ended as a tie, and most did. So, the league tried to reduce the number of ties beginning in the 1999–2000 season, with four skaters for each team (down from five) and a goalie. Both teams would be guaranteed one point, but the team that won in overtime would earn a second.

The rule changed again in 2005–06, when the shootout was introduced, and then in 2015, overtime was changed to a 3-on-3 format, which created more open ice, to limit shootouts.

So we move forward: here's another chance to eke out a win.

1 Only three teenagers made their NHL debuts as Rangers. Name them. *Answer on page 177.*

2 Before the shootout was introduced in 2005, perhaps the most fascinating segment during a game was the rare one-on-one duel between a skater and goaltender: the penalty shot, which is awarded when a player skating in on a breakaway is prevented from shooting by a pursuing opponent.

Who scored the first for the Rangers and which Rangers scored the most? *Answer on page 178.*

3 It's impossible to be a hard-core Rangers fan and not know when and how the rivalry with the Islanders started in the 1972–73 season. Who won the first exhibition game, the first regular-season game, and the season series? *Answer on page 179.*

4 I was the first player of Chinese descent to play in the NHL when I debuted with the Rangers in 1947. Who am I? *Answer on page 181.*

5 How many Rangers executives have won the GM of the Year Award and the Jack Adams Award for Coach of the Year? *Answer on page 183.*

6 Who was the only player from Nebraska to suit up for the Rangers? Hint: he is an amazing example of work ethic, dedication, and passion. *Answer on page 183.*

7 The transition from the 20th century to the 21st was not the brightest time for the franchise. For how many consecutive years did the Rangers fail to qualify for the playoffs? *Answer on page 185.*

8 A handful of Americans have stepped into the crease to play goal for the Rangers—from former Olympian Jack McCartan to Steve Baker to Mike Richter. But who was the first—and a native New Yorker at that—to stop pucks in an NHL game for the Blueshirts? *Answer on page 186.*

9 From 1927 to 2017, in which years did Rangers teams have their worst record in a single season? *Answer on page 187.*

OVERTIME—
ANSWERS

1 Don Raleigh, Dave Maloney, and John Vanbiesbrouck.

Raleigh, a 5-foot-11, 150-pound center, played 15 games as a 17-year-old in 1943–44, before suffering a broken jaw in a game against Toronto. He scored four points—two goals and two assists—wearing No. 7. Raleigh, who grew up in Manitoba, ended up skating in 535 games, with 101 goals and 320 points. On February 25, 1948, against the Chicago Black Hawks, he was the first player in Rangers history to score four goals in a game.

Maloney was 18 years, four months, and 18 days old when he was summoned from the Providence Reds and took his spot on defense on December 18, 1974, in a 7-0 victory over the Minnesota North Stars at Madison Square Garden. Maloney would later become the youngest captain in Rangers history, at 22, on October 11, 1978, inheriting the "C" from Phil Esposito.

Vanbiesbrouck, known as The Beezer, was 18 years and 93 days old when he played his first Rangers game on December 5, 1981, a 2-1 win over the Colorado Rockies on the road before he was returned to his junior team. He won the Vezina Trophy in 1985–86, and became the first player ever to dress for the Rangers, the New York Islanders, the New Jersey Devils, and the Philadelphia Flyers.

Defenseman Dave Maloney, the youngest captain in Rangers history at 22 and now a broadcaster, remains around the game. He and goalie Dan Blackburn were among the former Blueshirts playing in an alumni match against the Flyers on Dec. 31, 2011, in Philadelphia. (AP Photo/Tom Mihalek)

2 On January 16, 1936, Albert Patrick "Bert" Connelly tallied the first goal on a penalty shot, against Toronto's George Hainsworth, and it proved to be the winner as the Blueshirts defeated the Maple Leafs, 1-0, at Madison Square Garden. In an eerie coincidence, Connelly, who played for the Rangers for two seasons, was denied by Hainsworth almost a year earlier on January 31, 1935.

There were 76 penalty shots awarded to the Rangers between 1934 and the 2015–16 season. Players scored on 30 of them.

Only two Rangers have two penalty-shot goals: Alex Shibicky and Pavel Bure.

Shibicky is believed to be the first player to employ a slap shot, in 1937, which he said he learned from Fred "Bun" Cook in practice. He also was vice president of the first formation of the National Hockey League Players Association.

Bure, the Russian Rocket, was an electrifying skater and deadly shooter for the Vancouver Canucks and Florida Panthers before he came to the Rangers in 2001. In 12 games, he scored 12 goals and the following season, 19 in 39 games before knee problems ended his career.

Bure, of course, was on the wrong end of perhaps the greatest save in Rangers playoff history on a penalty shot when he was hooked by Brian Leetch in Game 4 of the Stanley Cup Final against the Canucks. He deked right and left but was stoned by Mike Richter's right pad as the Rangers held on to win.

Since 2007, the Rangers have had 27 penalty-shot opportunities. Only seven players scored: Jed Ortmeyer, Brendan Shanahan, Michal Rozsival, Sean Avery, Ryan Callahan, Derek Stepan, and Dan Boyle.

Boyle's score, on December 29, 2015, against Vancouver's Ryan Miller, was the only successful one of six in 2015–16: Chris Kreider missed twice and Jesper Fast, Keith Yandle, and Rick Nash each failed once.

3 The Rangers. They prevailed in the first exhibition match, 6-4, on September 27 at the Nassau Veterans Memorial Coliseum and the first regular season meeting with the Islanders, 2-1, also in Uniondale, on October 21, 1972. They also swept the season series, 6-0, by a combined score of 25-5.

Rod Gilbert's career was filled with too many shining moments to list here. But anybody remember Gilbert's first regular-season game against the Islanders? It was a hoot.

On October 21, 1972, the Coliseum was about 1,500 folks over capacity. Gilbert wasn't exactly a pacifist; goalie Billy Smith, however, took no prisoners.

The second period had barely started when the duo dropped the gloves. But the mask of "Battlin' Billy" remained lashed to his noggin. Rangers fans beseeched him to rid himself of the protection.

No opponent was welcome in either goal crease during the height of the Rangers-Islanders rivalry. As players tumble a few feet away, Rangers defenseman Pierre Plante tried to clear Billy Harris from in front of goalie John Davidson during a Stanley Cup playoff game at the Nassau Coliseum on May 5, 1979. (AP Photo/Ray Stubblebine)

After the 2-1 win, Gilbert was moaning: "How can I hit him? That's all I need is to break my hand." Smith deadpanned: "If I stop to take off my mask, the other guy could hit me."

Smith, who wound up with 42 penalty minutes that season, wasn't exactly a shrinking violet during the game—or any other. He also shoved and whacked and battled with wingers Pete Stemkowski and Glen Sather.

With far different casts on each side, that same 2-1 result bookended the Rangers-Isles rivalry at the Old Barn on March 10, 2015.

Anders Lee beat Cam Talbot in the first period, but Kevin Hayes and Rick Nash scored against Jaroslav Halak.

4 Larry Kwong's career with the Rangers was short-lived—one shift in one game in 1948—but that was enough to break a barrier.

Kwong's story was atypical for an immigrant Asian boy. His father brought the family to Vernon, British Columbia, from China in the 1880s to find a living in an area where gold was mined. But that venture failed and he farmed and opened a grocery store, Kwong Hing Lung.

The family's name was Eng, and adopted the name of the store when their father died. He and his brothers skated on a makeshift rink—an empty lot next door that they flooded with water.

He played in the town's midget league and later worked as a bellhop because he was denied employment at the town's smelter because of his ancestry, one taste of the discrimination of the era. But he was accepted by the Trail Smoke Eaters, a British Columbia junior team, and joined the Army during World War II.

It was when he played in hockey games to entertain the troops that he was spotted by a Rangers scout, who arranged a tryout in 1946 for the 5-foot-6 Kwong and he was assigned to the New York Rovers, the team's Eastern League affiliate, which also played at Madison Square Garden, then at 49th Street and Eighth Avenue.

"He was very clever and a good skater," veteran journalist Stan Fischler recalled. "He was like Yvan Cournoyer," the Montreal Canadiens forward of later years known as the "Roadrunner."

Before long, Kwong was heralded by the city's Chinese-American community, and was called the "China Clipper" and "King Kwong." Before one game, Shavey Lee, the unofficial mayor of Chinatown, and two showgirls from the China Doll nightclub honored him at center ice. He was 23.

In 1948, the Rangers were making a playoff run, but were ravaged by injuries, and Kwong and Rovers teammate Ronnie Rowe were summoned as substitutes and took a train to Montreal. On March 13, 1948, Kwong proudly dressed in the visitors locker room at the Montreal Forum, a dream realized.

It was a year after Jackie Robinson broke the Major League Baseball color line when the Brooklyn Dodgers started him at first base on April 15, 1947.

Rowe, also a forward, played regularly, but coach Frank Boucher kept Kwong on the bench through two periods, as the Rangers fell behind, 1-0. Late in the third period, with the score 2-2, Kwong went on the ice for one shift, and the Canadiens won 3-2.

"I was quite disappointed because I was only used for about a minute," he said. "I didn't get a real chance to show what I can do." Kwong did not question Boucher. "You didn't do that," he said. "He had his team."

"I don't think there was prejudice," Fischler would say, noting that Hub Anslow, Kwong's linemate, played only two games in the NHL. "I worked with Frank Boucher. He was a wonderful guy. But there was no justice for Larry Kwong. He deserved better."

Kwong quit the Rangers organization after the season. "I liked New York City very much," he said, "but when that happened, I said I'm going to a team that I knew wanted me in Quebec," and played seven years for the Valleyfield Braves. He finished his career in the minors.

In 2008, the Calgary Flames saluted him at the Saddledome in 2008, and he later was inducted into the British Columbia Sports Hall of Fame.

5 This one stings: none. General managers vote for the annual GM recognition; broadcasters vote for the Adams. And no player has ever won the Frank J. Selke Trophy, awarded to the best defensive forward.

6 Jed Ortmeyer, who was signed as a free agent in 2003 and courageously played through a series of injuries and life-threatening blood clots, was the only player from Nebraska to skate for the Blueshirts.

Ortmeyer's career began with the Omaha Lancers of the USHL in 1997, and continued at the University of Michigan from 1999 to 2003, where he tore his ACL as a sophomore, returned, and was named captain of the Wolverines as a junior.

He was not drafted, but the Rangers scouts and front office liked him and signed him in May 2003. That next season, he divided his time between New York and Hartford of the AHL, and debuted for the Blueshirts on November 15 against the Devils.

A fourth-line right wing and penalty-killer who never, ever took playing in the NHL for granted, Ortmeyer's career went sideways in August 2006, when he was diagnosed with a pulmonary embolism—blood clots in his lungs. He described his dismay—and passion for the game—in a stirring article for *The Players Tribune* in December 2016.

After the diagnosis, he was sidelined for four months before being cleared to play.

On January 13, 2007, in his sixth game since returning, he scored on a shorthanded penalty shot against the Boston Bruins in a 3-1 win. Sixteen days later, also against the Bruins, he contributed three assists and was named the game's first star. He was given the Steven McDonald Extra Effort Award in an overwhelming vote from Rangers fans, and was nominated for the Bill Masterton Memorial Trophy for dedication and perseverance.

He was already injecting himself with blood thinners daily in order to keep playing, but after signing a two-year contract with Nashville, he ruptured an ACL again, and more blood clots formed during surgery. A filter had to be placed in his chest to prevent any future clots traveling to his major organs, and rehabbed for a year. Ortmeyer then played another six years in the NHL and in the AHL. He retired when he and his wife had their first child, and the couple ran a company that helped athletes transition into new careers. In June 2017, he was named the Rangers director of player development.

7 The Blueshirts playoff drought around the millennium lasted seven seasons: 1998, 1999, 2000, 2001, 2002, 2003, and 2004. It was the longest stretch in team history.

They also missed for consecutive seasons from 1943 through 1947, 1950 through 1956, 1959 through 1961, 1963 through 1966, and in 1976 and 1977.

Of course, winning four Stanley Cups are the franchise's playoff highlights.

Here are five of many, many forgotten great dates from early rounds in the playoffs:

May 3, 2012. Marian Gaborik's goal in the third overtime in Washington past Braden Holtby downs the Capitals, 2-1 in Game 3 of the Eastern Conference semifinals in the franchise's longest game in 73 years.

April 23, 1997. At age 36 Wayne Gretzky's hat trick—a natural one, in a 6:23 time span—leads the Rangers to a 3-2 win over Florida in Game 4 and the Blueshirts wrap up the series in five on Esa Tikkanen's goal two days later.

May 12, 1995. Brian Leetch backhands a shot past Quebec goalie Stephane Fiset at 12:42 of overtime to give the Rangers a 4-3 win in the Game 3 of the conference quarter-finals, and the Rangers go on to oust the Nordiques in six games.

April 18, 1994. Mike Richter becomes the first goalie to win back-to-back playoff shutouts since Davey Kerr in 1940, in a 6-0 whitewash of the Islanders.

April 15, 1971. In Game 6 of the Stanley Cup Quarter-finals, Bob Nevin scores at 9:07 of overtime to lift the Rangers to a 2-1 win over the Maple Leafs. It was the team's first playoff series win in 21 years.

8 Joe Schaefer, a Long Island office-supply manager and former amateur goaltender who was summoned as the emergency replacement for Gump Worsley for a game against the Chicago Blackhawks in 1960.

NHL teams only carried and dressed one goaltender until the rules changed in 1965. Each home team was required to have an emergency substitute in the stands if either teams' keep was injured and could not play. Canadian teams often had a junior team goalie available, but not so in the US.

Schaefer, 35, was a part-time jack-of-all-trades for the Rangers: a statistician, assistant trainer, practice netminder, goal judge, and penalty-box timekeeper during the 1950s. His hockey background? The Sands Point (Long Island) Tigers of the Metropolitan Amateur Hockey League, which also fielded teams in Brooklyn, Manhattan, Queens, the Bronx, Westchester County, and New Jersey during its existence.

But Schaefer's moment in the sun came on February 17, 1960, when Bobby Hull's skate sliced Worsley's stick-hand glove in the first minute of the second period, a cut that damaged some tendons.

After a 23-minute delay, Schaefer, who was 5-foot-8 and 165 pounds, emerged from the dressing room to face the Hawks. "He turned white when he was told to get into uniform," Worsley recalled in his autobiography. The Rangers led 1-0 at the time, but although Schaefer made 17 saves, the Hawks won 5-1. According to the *New York Times*, "Schaefer had little to offer except courage." He was paid $100 for his valiant performance.

In an eerie coincidence, Schaefer made a second appearance, on March 8, 1961, after another Worsley-Hull incident. Stretching to stop Hull's wrist shot, Worsley tore his hamstring and was stretchered off the ice halfway through the first period with the score tied at 1.

Schaefer made 27 saves, but the Rangers lost 4-3. While in the hospital, Worsley received a post-game visit from Schaefer, who was still shaken by the experience. "Stay healthy Gumpy, will you please?" Schaefer pleaded, Worsley recalled.

To his relief, before retiring as a statistician in 1986, Schaefer was never called on again.

His final Rangers stats? Two games played (86 minutes), a 5.58 goals against average and an 0-2-0 record. But that was enough to earn him a spot on the list of US goalies who suited up for the Rangers, which also includes McCartan, a 1960 Olympian who played his first game as a Ranger on March 6, 1960, Baker, Richter, Mike Dunham, Guy Hebert, Scott Meyer, and John Vanbiesbrouck.

Note: another Rangers practice goalie in that era was Arnie Nocks, a New York City native, who was a player-coach with the New Jersey Rockets, and a director for ABC's Eyewitness News, The Soupy Sales Show, and other programs.

9 Because the Rangers played different schedules over the years, we'll have to break them up, according to the number of games played in a season.

In 1943–44, when NHL players were serving in the military during World War II, the Rangers were 6-39-5, for 17 points in 50 games.

During the era when the NHL played 70 games per season, the Rangers went 18-41-11 in 1965–66, for 47 points.

In 1984–85, when the league had increased the number of games to 80, the Rangers posted 62 points (26-44-10).

THE SHOOTOUT

It's down to skill now. Sixty-five minutes are in the books. One-on-one. Shooter against goaltender for the extra point.

The shootout, which much of the media and some coaches call a gimmick that doesn't rely on teamwork to determine a winner, can last as many rounds as necessary until one team scores more goals.

But given the 82-game schedule and the travel involved, games have to end at a reasonable hour. In fact, most end in three rounds. And fans are generally standing for the evening's finale.

So we'll give you three questions and then be on our way . . . .

1 On November 26, 2005, the Rangers and Capitals participated in a 15-round shootout (the longest in NHL history at the time), which ended with Marek Malik's between-the-legs goal to give the Rangers a 3-2 win at the Garden. Who were the other Rangers shootout scorers in this classic battle? *Answer on page 191.*

2 In what year were these players and their numbers listed on a Rangers roster: Wasson, 22; Kangarpool, 44; Kocreko, 10; and Yeaton, 13? Can you solve this mystery? *Answer on page 192.*

3 Okay, back to real life. Who had the assist on Stephane Matteau's double-overtime goal that eliminated the Devils and clinched the 1994 trip to the Stanley Cup Final? *Answer on page 193.*

THE SHOOTOUT—
ANSWERS

1 Michael Nylander, Ville Nieminen, and Jason Strudwick.

The deciding goal by Malik, a 30-year-old Czech defenseman in his first season with the Rangers, is an indelible memory and the defining moment in his career. After all, the unlikely hero had scored just 27 goals in parts of 10 seasons to that point.

Of course, Malik's magical moment at Madison Square Garden would never have taken place if not for Nylander, Nieminen, Strudwick, and a rookie goalie named Henrik Lundqvist.

With the Rangers and Washington Capitals tied 2-2, the shootout began with another rookie, Alex Ovechkin, being stopped by Lundqvist. Nylander scored in the second round on a high, glove-side backhander past goalie Olaf Kolzig to tie the event at 1-1. It was no surprise that Rangers coach Tom Renney sent Nylander out early. The slick Swedish center had been an annual double-digit scorer for his three previous teams, the Calgary Flames, Chicago Blackhawks, and the Caps.

In the sixth round, right wing Brian Willsie beat Lundqvist to make the score 2-1. Nieminen, a Finnish left wing who had won the Stanley Cup with the Colorado Avalanche in 2001, jumped over the boards and skated to center ice. His wrister went past Kolzig's arm, and sent a ripple through the sold-out crown and the benches.

"At that point in time, we started to feel we were looking at something pretty special," Renney said. "We sat back and watched as the event unfolded." Said Lundqvist: "I started to think it would never end."

Finally in Round 14, Caps defenseman Brian Muir wired a wrist shot past Lundqvist's stick arm. Running out of options, Renney chose to use defenseman Jason Strudwick to try to score, or the marathon would be over. "I never really thought I would have to shoot in a shootout," Strudwick recalled. "In fact, I think some of my teammates were already in the dressing room."

But the 6-foot-4 Strudwick, who would finish his career with just 13 goals in 674 NHL games, didn't deke or try to fool Kolzig. He skated straight in and launched a wrister that snuck between Kolzig's arm and body.

Lundqvist then denied Matt Bradley, and Renney motioned to Malik, who had 27 career goals in parts of 10 NHL seasons with Carolina, Hartford, and Vancouver. Kolzig later said, "I was thinking about who they were going to use after Marek."

Malik slowly skated in and it appeared he was going to try a backhand shot. Instead, he pulled the stick between his legs and roofed the puck over Kolzig's right shoulder. The surprise move delighted the crowd and the benches.

"I was the one who made that shot, and it really makes me happy," Malik said when he retired. "Lots of people tell me that when they have a bad day, they go on YouTube and look at the goal and they get in a better mood. That's that thing that makes me even happier."

2 Don't start checking the record books. These Rangers never appeared in an NHL or AHL game.

Perhaps the last word of the question was too much of a giveaway.

In this case, the Rangers and the rest of the game's roster is fictional. They are the players in the 1999 movie *Mystery, Alaska*, which starred Russell Crowe and Burt Reynolds.

Mystery is a small town where the weekly Saturday Game of four-on-four pond hockey is played on the town's frozen lake, and is the subject of a fictional *Sports Illustrated* article. A nationally televised exhibition game is scheduled between the Rangers and the 10-man local team, which takes a 2-0 lead early. Sound familiar, Rangers fans?

In the second period, the Rangers score five unanswered goals, but Mystery fights back and scores twice in the third. As time ticks down, a Mystery player's shot hits the cross-bar, and they lose, 5-4. Even the Rangers players applaud the effort.

3 Esa Tikkanen.

Of all people, it was the motor-mouth pest from Helsinki, called "The Grate One," who was credited with the helper on one of the most famous scores in franchise history.

Tikkanen, the son of a boxer, was a hard-nosed wing who became a Ranger when 22-year-old Doug Weight was sent to the Edmonton Oilers on March 17, 1993.

The distracting—and irritating—yapper played on the same squad with the legit "Great One" Wayne Gretzky, scored 30 goals three times, and was on five Stanley Cup teams. His colorful stream of taunting was a maddening blend of Finnish, Swedish, English, and made-up words, teammates recalled, that was often indecipherable.

In the 1990 postseason, Tikkanen scored 13 goals and had 11 assists when the Oilers won the Cup and shadowed Gretzky, then with the Los Angeles Kings.

"He brings something special," Gretzky said. "I don't know what it is, but if you ask him, you wouldn't understand the answer."

In that decisive Rangers game, a deflection off Tikkanen forced the puck into the left corner of the Devils' zone. Matteau, who had won Game 3 of the series with a double-overtime goal, swept in and beat Scott Niedermeyer to the loose puck. Matteau then carried the puck behind the Devils' cage and emerged on the other side, where defenseman Slava Fetisov charged at him. Matteau's wraparound went off Martin Brodeur's stick and over the goal line at 4:24 of the second overtime.

Tikkanen also scored an overtime playoff goal for the Rangers against Florida three years later, but it was that assist on a goal in 1994 that changed the fortunes of a franchise that gave people—and Tikkanen—something else to talk about for years.

"Esa talks twice as much as anybody else," said former teammate Craig MacTavish. "That's because you can understand only half of what he says."

All right, congratulations, and many thanks for playing along. You've proved your mettle as a diehard Rangers fan.

As a reward, think of the message on the blackboard in the classic photo of Toronto Maple Leafs Punch Imlach in his office in 1963. Imlach is in shirt and tie, legs up and sipping champagne with the Stanley Cup on a nearby table. The blackboard reads, "No Practice Tomorrow."